PHP Design Pattern

Essentials

PHP Design Pattern

Essentials

Tony Bevis

Ability First Limited
Essex, United Kingdom

AbilityFIRST

PHP Design Pattern Essentials

British Library Cataloguing in Publication Data. A catalogue record for this book is available from the British Library.

Publishing history:

- First edition, October 2013

Published by:

Ability First Limited

Dragon Enterprise Centre, 28 Stephenson Road

Leigh-on-Sea, Essex SS9 5LY, United Kingdom

www.abilityfirst.co.uk/books

ISBN: 978-0-9565758-8-3

Cover image by Ivan Polushkin, copyright Fotolia.

This book is dedicated to

"The Gang of Four"

Table of Contents

Preface

This book is an introductory guide to the world of object-oriented software design patterns. The examples and code extracts have been deliberately kept simple, allowing you to concentrate on understanding the concepts and application of each pattern rather than having to wade through irrelevant source code.

The book assumes that you have at least a basic knowledge of the PHP programming language, including understanding what is meant by the terms encapsulation, inheritance and polymorphism, and that you know how to write classes and interfaces. By the end of this book you should be able to apply that knowledge to the design of complex applications, where objects from multiple classes need to interact to accomplish particular goals.

The patterns described within comprise all 23 of the patterns in the seminal work of Erich Gamma, Richard Helm, Ralph Johnson and John Vlissides; *Design Patterns: Elements of Reusable Object-Oriented Software* (Addison-Wesley, 1995). There are also three additional patterns described including Model-View-Controller (MVC), now a mainstay of graphical applications. For the most part, each chapter is self-contained, and you can therefore dip into the patterns in any order. However, it is recommended that you read Chapter 1 *"What are Design Patterns?"* first to familiarise yourself with the common theme and the object-oriented principles that the patterns utilise.

This book also makes use of a simplified implementation of Unified Modeling Language (UML) diagrams to show how the classes that comprise a pattern are structured. If you are unfamiliar with UML diagrams then you may wish to refer to Appendix A before you begin.

Prerequisite knowledge

In order to make use of this book you should have a basic understanding of both the PHP language and of object-oriented principles. In particular, you should know how to create classes and interfaces, and understand the terms encapsulation, inheritance, composition and polymorphism.

How this book is organised

Part I introduces the idea of design patterns, and lays the foundation for some simple core classes that comprise the common theme used throughout this book.

Part II describes the five creational patterns, that is, those that help manage the instantiation of objects.

Part III describes the seven structural patterns, that is, those that help manage how classes are organised and interrelate.

Part IV describes the eleven behavioural patterns, that is, those that help manage what the classes actually do.

Part V describes three additional patterns you should find useful in practical applications.

Part VI contains the appendixes, which includes a brief explanation of the Unified Modeling Language (UML) diagram formats for those unfamiliar with UML, and a quick reference for each of the 23 main patterns.

Conventions used in this book

PHP code that you need to enter, or results that are shown as output, is shown in a fixed-width font as follows:

```
$anObject->doSomething();
$anotherObject->doThis();
```

Often, a piece of additional or modified code is provided, and the parts that are new or changed are indicated in **bold**:

```
$anObject->doSomethingElseInstead();
$anObject->alsoDoThis();
$anotherObject->doThis();
```

Names of classes, objects or PHP statements will appear in the text using a fixed-width font such as `MyClass` or `$someObject`, for example.

Where some useful or important additional information about a topic is included it will be shown in a note-box, like the following:

This is some additional information in a note-box.

For reasons of brevity, `include`, `include_once`, `require` and `require_once` statements are omitted from most of the code samples in this book.

The book's resources

You can also download all of the PHP source code from this book from our website:

http://www.abilityfirst.co.uk/books

Note to readers

This book is an adaptation of *Java Design Pattern Essentials - Second Edition* by the same author. It is possible that some of the text and code samples may reflect this adaptation in terms of the style and terminology differences between the languages. Readers' feedback is more than welcome.

Part I.   Introduction

This part introduces the idea of design patterns, and lays the foundation for some simple core classes that comprise the common theme used throughout this book.

- What are Design Patterns?

1.   What are Design Patterns?

Imagine that you have just been assigned the task of designing a software system. Your customer tells you that he needs to model the Gadgets his factory makes and that each Gadget comprises the same component parts but those parts are a bit different for each type of Gadget. And he also makes Gizmos, where each Gizmo comes with a selection of optional extras any combination of which can be chosen. And he also needs a unique sequential serial number stamped on each item made.

Just how would you go about designing these classes?

The chances are that no matter what problem domain you are working in, somebody else has had to design a similar solution in the past. Not necessarily for Gadgets and Gizmos of course, but conceptually similar in terms of objectives and structure. In other words there's a good chance that a generic solution or approach already exists, and all you need to do is to apply that approach to solve your design conundrum.

This is what *Design Patterns* are for. They describe generic solutions to software design problems. Once versed in patterns, you might think to yourself "those Gadgets could be modelled using the *Abstract Factory* pattern, the Gizmos using the *Decorator* pattern, and the serial number generation using the *Singleton* pattern."

How this book uses patterns

This book gives worked examples for each of the 23 patterns described in the classic reference work *Design Patterns – Elements of Reusable Object-Oriented Software* (Gamma, 1995) plus three additional useful patterns, including Model-View-Controller (MVC).

Each of the worked examples in this book uses a common theme drawn from the business world, being that of a fictional vehicle manufacturer called the Foobar Motor Company. The company makes a range of cars and vans together with the engines used to power the vehicles. You should therefore familiarise yourself with the classes described in this introduction.

The class hierarchy looks like this:

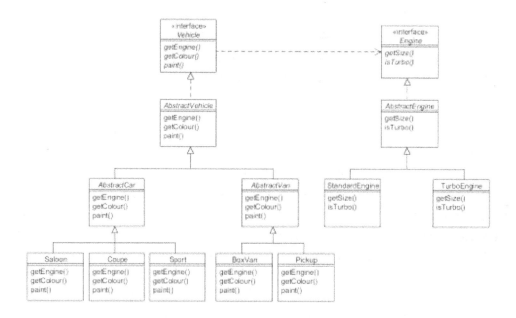

Figure 1.1 : Vehicle and Engine class hierarchies

Vehicle and Engine are the root interfaces of the hierarchies, with each vehicle object requiring a reference to an Engine object. AbstractVehicle is an abstract class that implements the Vehicle interface, and AbstractEngine likewise implements the Engine interface. For vehicles, we also have AbstractCar and AbstractVan together with concrete subclassses Saloon, Coupe and Sport as types of cars. AbstractVan has the concrete subclasses BoxVan and Pickup as types of van.

The concrete subclasses of AbstractEngine are StandardEngine and TurboEngine.

Despite there being several classes in the hierarchies the code for each has been kept deliberately simple so you can focus on understanding the patterns rather than having to decipher complex code. To illustrate this, here is the PHP source code for the Engine interface:

engine.php

```php
<?php
interface Engine {
    public function getSize();
    public function isTurbo();
}
?>
```

This simple interface merely requires function getters to return the engine size (in cubic centimetres) and whether it is turbocharged.

The AbstractEngine class looks like this:

abstract_engine.php

```php
<?php
abstract class AbstractEngine implements Engine {

    private $size;
    private $turbo;

    public function __construct($size, $turbo) {
        $this->size = $size;
        $this->turbo = $turbo;
    }

    public function getSize() {
        return $this->size;
    }

    public function isTurbo() {
        return $this->turbo;
    }

    public function __toString() {
        return get_class($this) . '(' . (string)$this->size . ')';
    }
}
?>
```

This simplified implementation of an engine requires the appropriate attributes to be supplied in the constructor. The __toString() function has been implemented to produce output in this format:

```
StandardEngine (1300)
TurboEngine (2000)
```

The concrete subclasses are trivially simple:

standard_engine.php

```php
<?php
class StandardEngine extends AbstractEngine {

    public function __construct($size) {
        parent::__construct($size, false); // not turbocharched
    }

}
?>
```

turbo_engine.php

```php
<?php
class TurboEngine extends AbstractEngine {

    public function __construct($size) {
        parent::__construct($size, true); // turbocharched
    }

}
?>
```

Now that you have seen the Engine hierarchy we can look at the Vehicle interface:

vehicle.php

```php
<?php
interface Vehicle {

    const UNPAINTED   = "Unpainted";
    const BLUE        = "Blue";
    const BLACK       = "Black";
    const GREEN       = "Green";
    const RED         = "Red";
```

```php
    const SILVER        = "Silver";
    const WHITE         = "White";
    const YELLOW        = "Yellow";

    public function getEngine();
    public function getColour();
    public function paint($colour);
}
?>
```

A small number of constants define the possible colours that each Vehicle object could be.

This is how the AbstractVehicle class implements Vehicle:

abstract_vehicle.php

```php
<?php
abstract class AbstractVehicle implements Vehicle {

    private $engine;
    private $colour;

    public function __construct(Engine $engine,
                                $colour = Vehicle::UNPAINTED) {
        $this->engine = $engine;
        $this->colour = $colour;
    }

    public function getEngine() {
        return $this->engine;
    }

    public function getColour() {
        return $this->colour;
    }

    public function paint($colour) {
        $this->colour = $colour;
    }

    public function __toString() {
        return get_class($this) . '(' .
                (string)$this->engine . ', ' .
                (string)$this->colour . ')';
    }
}
?>
```

The constructor in `AbstractVehicle` requires an `Engine` object and optionally a vehicle colour to be supplied.

The output of calls to `__toString()` will be in this format:

```
Saloon (StandardEngine (1300), Red)
BoxVan (TurboEngine (2200), White)
```

The `AbstractCar` and `AbstractVan` classes just forward to the constructors (obviously real classes would define whatever is different between cars and vans):

abstract_car.php

```php
<?php
abstract class AbstractCar extends AbstractVehicle {

    public function __construct(Engine $engine,
                                $colour = Vehicle::UNPAINTED) {
        parent::__construct($engine, $colour);
    }
}
?>
```

abstract_van.php

```php
<?php
abstract class AbstractVan extends AbstractVehicle {

    public function __construct(Engine $engine,
                                $colour = Vehicle::UNPAINTED) {
        parent::__construct($engine, $colour);
    }
}
?>
```

The concrete subclasses also just forward to the constructors:

saloon.php

```php
<?php
class Saloon extends AbstractCar {

    public function __construct(Engine $engine,
                                $colour = Vehicle::UNPAINTED) {
```

```php
            parent::__construct($engine, $colour);
        }
    }
    ?>
```

coupe.php

```php
    <?php
    class Coupe extends AbstractCar {

        public function __construct(Engine $engine,
                                    $colour = Vehicle::UNPAINTED) {
            parent::__construct($engine, $colour);
        }
    }
    ?>
```

sport.php

```php
    <?php
    class Sport extends AbstractCar {

        public function __construct(Engine $engine,
                                    $colour = Vehicle::UNPAINTED) {
            parent::__construct($engine, $colour);
        }
    }
    ?>
```

boxvan.php

```php
    <?php
    class BoxVan extends AbstractVan {

        public function __construct(Engine $engine,
                                    $colour = Vehicle::UNPAINTED) {
            parent::__construct($engine, $colour);
        }
    }
    ?>
```

pickup.php

```php
    <?php
    class Pickup extends AbstractVan {

        public function __construct(Engine $engine,
                                    $colour = Vehicle::UNPAINTED) {
```

```
        parent::__construct($engine, $colour);
    }
}
?>
```

Many of the patterns in this book utilise one or more of the above classes in some way, often adding additional functionality or classes for the purposes of explaining the pattern in question. You will also frequently see reference to a `Client` class; this just refers to whatever class is making use of the pattern under discussion: in the examples in this book this will usually be `index.php`.

How patterns are categorised

Each of the patterns described in this book fall under one of three categories; *Creational, Structural* or *Behavioural*:

- *Creational* patterns provide approaches to object instantiation. Where you place the `new` keyword affects how tightly or loosely coupled your classes are;

- *Structural* patterns provide approaches for combining classes and objects to form larger structures. Deciding whether to use inheritance or composition affects how flexible and adaptable your software is;

- *Behavioural* patterns provide approaches for handling communication between objects.

Common principles in design patterns

Experience has shown that some object-oriented approaches are more flexible than others. Here is a summary of the main principles that the patterns in this book strive to adhere to:

1. ***Program to an interface, not an implementation.*** By "interface" is meant the general concept of abstraction, which could refer to a PHP interface or an abstract class. To accomplish this, use the most general type (e.g. interface) possible when declaring variables, constructor and function arguments, etc. Doing so gives extra flexibility as to the actual types that are used at run-time.

2. ***Prefer object composition over inheritance.*** Where a class is related to another in some way, you should distinguish between "is a" (or "is a type of") and "has a" relationships. In the `Vehicle` and `Engine` hierarchies described earlier, it is true to say that `AbstractCar` "is a" `Vehicle`, and that `Saloon` "is a" `AbstractCar`. But it would not be true to say that `Vehicle` "is a" `Engine`, but rather that a `Vehicle` "has a" `Engine`. Therefore, inheritance is legitimately used for `AbstractCar` and `Saloon`, but object composition is used between `Vehicle` and `Engine`. Do not be tempted to use inheritance just to save having to write some functions. Sometimes using a "has a" relationship is more flexible even when an "is a" relationship seems the natural choice. You will see an example of this in the *Decorator* pattern.

3. ***Keep objects loosely-coupled.*** Ideally, classes should model just one thing, and only be composed of other objects that are genuinely required (such as a `Vehicle` requiring an `Engine`). Ask yourself what would happen if you wanted to use a class you have written in a completely different application; what "baggage" (i.e. other classes) would also need to be copied? By keeping this to a minimum, you make your class more re-usable. A good example of a pattern that uses loose-coupling is *Observer*.

4. ***Encapsulate the concept that varies.*** If you've written a class in which some parts are the same for each instance but another part of the class varies for each instance, consider extracting the latter into a class of its own, which is referenced by the original class. An example pattern that uses principle is *Strategy*.

Some general advice

The principles listed above will become more apparent as we explore the patterns in detail. You should also note that the patterns described in this book give a general approach to a particular problem. It is quite acceptable for you to modify or adapt them to better fit your particular problem. And it is very common for multiple patterns to be combined to solve complex problems.

However, do remember that you should strive to keep things simple. It is easy, after reading a book such as this, to think that you have to find a pattern to solve a particular problem when an even simpler solution might be available. One of the mantras of Extreme Programming (XP) is "You aren't going to need it", the idea being that you should avoid adding features before they are required, and this philosophy could also be applied to patterns – beware of adding an unnecessary feature just so you can apply a pattern. Patterns are not a "magic bullet", just another set of tools in your toolkit, albeit an indispensable set.

Use your knowledge and experience to judge whether a pattern should be applied to your circumstances, and if so to what extent you need to adapt it. A good example of when applying patterns may be beneficial is when you are "refactoring" existing code. Refactoring is when you are changing the structure of some software but not its behaviour, to improve its maintainability and flexibility. This provides a good opportunity to examine your code to see if a pattern might provide a better structure, such as replacing conditionals, or defining factory classes to aid object instantiation.

Patterns have been applied to many programming languages besides PHP, particularly object-oriented languages, and indeed other fields, having originated by being applied to architectural design. And new patterns are being developed and applied on a regular basis, so you may view this book as merely a starting point in the subject.

Part II. Creational Patterns

This part describes the five creational patterns, that is, those that help manage the instantiation of objects.

- *Abstract Factory*: Provide an interface for creating families of related or dependent objects without specifying their concrete classes;

- *Builder*: Separate the construction of a complex object from its representation so that the same construction process can create different representations;

- *Factory Method*: Define an interface for creating an object, but let subclasses decide which class to instantiate;

- *Prototype*: Specify the kinds of objects to create using a prototypical instance, and create new objects by copying the prototype;

- *Singleton*: Ensure a class allows only one object to be created, providing a single point of access to it.

2. Abstract Factory

Type	Creational
Purpose	Provide an interface for creating families of related or dependent objects without specifying their concrete classes.

The Foobar Motor Company makes cars and vans, which when being built comprises (among lots of other things) a body shell, a chassis and glassware for the windows. Although both cars and vans need all of the same types of components, the specifics of each type differ depending upon whether it is being used for a car or a van.

In other words:

- *A car's body shell is different from a van's body shell;*

- *A car's chassis is different from a van's chassis;*

- *A car's windows are different from a van's windows.*

Therefore, when we need to build a vehicle we can think of the components as coming from different 'families'; that is, when we build a car we use one family of components and when we build a van we use a different family of components.

We can thus model the components into simple hierarchies, as illustrated in the following figure:

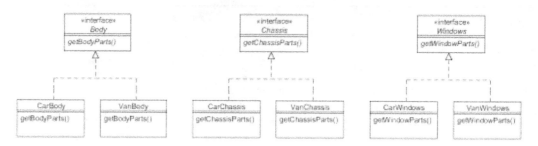

Figure 2.1 : Body, Chassis & Windows class hierarchies

As you can see, there is an interface for `Body` having implementations of `CarBody` and `VanBody`. Likewise we have similar separate hierarchies for `Chassis` and `Windows`.

The code for the `Body` hierarchy is very simple:

body.php

```
interface Body {
    public function getBodyParts();
}
```

car_body.php

```
class CarBody implements Body {

    public function getBodyParts() {
        return 'Body shell parts for a car';
    }

}
```

van_body.php

```
class VanBody implements Body {

    public function getBodyParts() {
        return 'Body shell parts for a van';
    }
```

```
    }
```

The code for the `Chassis` hierarchy is almost identical:

chassis.php

```
interface Chassis {
    public function getChassisParts();
}
```

car_chassis.php

```
class CarChassis implements Chassis {

    public function getChassisParts() {
        return 'Chassis parts for a car';
    }

}
```

van_chassis.php

```
class VanChassis implements Chassis {

    public function getChassisParts() {
        return 'Chassis parts for a van';
    }

}
```

And likewise the code for the `Windows` hierarchy:

windows.php

```
interface Windows {
    public function getWindowParts();
}
```

car_windows.php

```
class CarWindows implements Windows {

    public function getWindowParts() {
```

```
        return 'Window glassware for a car';
    }

}
```

van_windows.php

```
class VanWindows implements Windows {

    public function getWindowParts() {
        return 'Window glassware for a van';
    }

}
```

Now we need a way of getting the correct family of parts (either for a car or for a van) but without having to explicitly instantiate the specific type in client programs each time we require them. To accomplish this, we shall define "factory" classes that will do this for us:

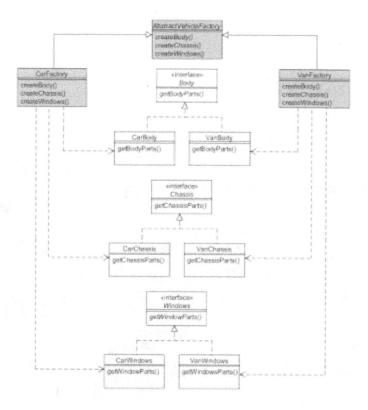

Figure 2.2 Abstract Factory

The `AbstractVehicleFactory` class is an abstract class that defines the abstract functions `createBody()`, `createChassis()` and `createWindows()`, returning a `Body`, `Chassis` and `Windows` object respectively:

abstract_vehicle_factory.php

```
abstract class AbstractVehicleFactory {
    public abstract function createBody();
    public abstract function createChassis();
    public abstract function createWindows();
}
```

The concrete subclass `CarFactory` returns the objects specific for the `Car` family:

car_factory.php

```
class CarFactory extends AbstractVehicleFactory {

    public function createBody() {
        return new CarBody();
    }

    public function createChassis() {
        return new CarChassis();
    }

    public function createWindows() {
        return new CarWindows();
    }
}
```

The concrete subclass `VanFactory` returns the objects specific for the `Van` family:

van_factory.php

```
class VanFactory extends AbstractVehicleFactory {

    public function createBody() {
        return new VanBody();
    }

    public function createChassis() {
        return new VanChassis();
```

```
    }

    public function createWindows() {
        return new VanWindows();
    }
}
```

Now it just remains for client programs to instantiate the appropriate 'factory' after which it can obtain the correct parts without having to specify whether they are for a car or a van:

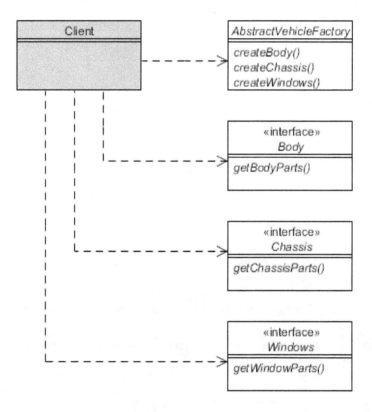

Figure 2.3 : How clients use Abstract Factory

```
$what_to_make = "car"; // or "van"
```

```php
// Create the correct 'factory'...
if ($what_to_make == 'car'):
    $factory = new CarFactory();
else:
    $factory = new VanFactory();
endif;

// Create the vehicle's component parts...
// These will either be all car parts or all van parts.
$vehicle_body = $factory->createBody();
$vehicle_chassis = $factory->createChassis();
$vehicle_windows = $factory->createWindows();

// Show what we've created (e.g. in the HTML section)...
<p><?php echo $vehicle_body->getBodyParts(); ?></p>
<p><?php echo $vehicle_chassis->getChassisParts(); ?></p>
<p><?php echo $vehicle_windows->getWindowParts(); ?></p>
```

Therefore your client program needs to know if it is making a car or a van, but once it has instantiated the correct factory all the functions to create the parts can be done using an identical set of function calls.

The main disadvantage of the *Abstract Factory* pattern arises if you need to add additional 'products'. For example, if we now need to include Lights in the family of components, we would need to amend AbstractVehicleFactory, CarFactory and VanFactory, in addition to creating a new Lights hierarchy (CarLights and VanLights).

3. Builder

Type	Creational
Purpose	Separate the construction of a complex object from its representation so that the same construction process can create different representations.

The Foobar Motor Company makes cars and vans, and the construction process of each differs in detail; for example, the body shell of a van comprises a cab area and a large reinforced storage area, whereas a saloon car comprises a passenger area and a luggage area (i.e. boot). And of course there a number of complex steps that have to be undertaken regardless of what type of vehicle is being built.

The *Builder* pattern facilitates the construction of complex objects by separating the individual steps into separate functions in a *Builder* hierarchy, and then using a *Director* object to specify the required steps in the correct order. Finally, the finished product is retrieved from the *Builder*.

The following diagram shows these relationships:

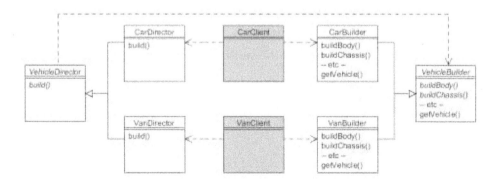

Figure 3.1 : Builder pattern

We start off with the abstract `VehicleBuilder` class:

vehicle_builder.php

```
abstract class VehicleBuilder {
    public function buildBody() {}
    public function buildBoot() {}
    public function buildChassis() {}
    public function buildPassengerArea() {}
    public function buildReinforcedStorageArea() {}
    public function buildWindows() {}

    public abstract function getVehicle();
}
```

Note how this class defines all possible 'build' functions for both cars and vans, and provides empty implementations for each as a default. The abstract `getVehicle()` function is for returning the finished vehicle.

The `CarBuilder` class inherits from `VehicleBuilder` and overrides the appropriate functions:

car_builder.php

```
class CarBuilder extends VehicleBuilder {

    private $carInProgress;

    public __construct(AbstractCar $abstract_car) {
        $this->carInProgress = $abstract_car;
    }

    public function buildBody() {
        // Add body to $this->carInProgress
    }

    public function buildBoot() {
        // Add boot to $this->carInProgress
    }

    public function buildChassis() {
        // Add chassis to $this->carInProgress
    }

    public function buildPassengerArea() {
        // Add passenger area to $this->carInProgress
    }
```

```
    public function buildWindows() {
        // Add windows to $this->carInProgress
    }

    public function getVehicle() {
        return $this->carInProgress;
    }

}
```

Note that the `buildReinforcedStorageArea()` function was not overridden since it is not applicable to cars.

The `VanBuilder` class overrides the appropriate functions to build a van:

van_builder.php

```
class VanBuilder extends VehicleBuilder {

    private $vanInProgress;

    public __construct(AbstractVan $abstract_van) {
        $this->vanInProgress = $abstract_van;
    }

    public function buildBody() {
        // Add body to $this->vanInProgress
    }

    public function buildChassis() {
        // Add chassis to $this->vanInProgress
    }

    public function buildReinforcedStorageArea() {
        // Add storage area to $this->vanInProgress
    }

    public function buildWindows() {
        // Add windows to $this->vanInProgress
    }

    public function getVehicle() {
        return $this->vanInProgress;
    }

}
```

Note that the `buildBoot()` and `buildPassengerArea()` functions were not overridden since they are not applicable to vans.

The `VehicleDirector` abstract class requires a `VehicleBuilder` object passed to its `build()` function for implementation by subclasses:

vehicle_director.php

```
abstract class VehicleDirector {
    public abstract function build(VehicleBuilder $vehicle_builder);
}
```

The `CarDirector` class inherits from `VehicleDirector` and provides the step-by-step process for building a car:

car_director.php

```
class CarDirector extends VehicleDirector {

    public function build(VehicleBuilder $vehicle_builder) {
        $vehicle_builder->buildChassis();
        $vehicle_builder->buildBody();
        $vehicle_builder->buildPassengerArea();
        $vehicle_builder->buildBoot();
        $vehicle_builder->buildWindows();

        return $vehicle_builder->getVehicle();
    }

}
```

The `VanDirector` class provides the step-by-step process for building a van:

van_director.php

```
class VanDirector extends VehicleDirector {

    public function build(VehicleBuilder $vehicle_builder) {
        $vehicle_builder->buildChassis();
        $vehicle_builder->buildBody();
        $vehicle_builder->buildReinforcedStorageArea();
        $vehicle_builder->buildWindows();
```

```
        return $vehicle_builder->getVehicle();
    }

}
```

As an example of how to use the above classes, let's assume we want to build a `Saloon` car:

```
$car = new Saloon(new StandardEngine(1300));
$builder = new CarBuilder($car);
$director = new CarDirector();
$vehicle = $director->build($builder);
```

You can see the required *Builder* object is constructed and passed to the required *Director* object, after which we invoke the function to build the product and then retrieve the finished article. The output should show:

```
Saloon (StandardEngine (1300), Unpainted)
```

4.   Factory Method

Type	Creational
Purpose	Define an interface for creating an object, but let subclasses decide which class to instantiate.

You will recall from the introduction the following class hierarchy for the vehicles made by the Foobar Motor Company:

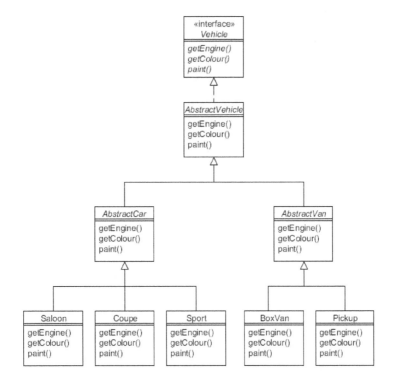

Figure 4.1 : Vehicle class hierarchy

When we need to instantiate a particular type of vehicle (such as a Coupe) it is often more flexible to define a separate class whose responsibility it is to manage the instantiation. This separate class is known as a *Factory*.

The *Factory Method* pattern defines an abstract class which serves as the 'factory' and that has an abstract function within to determine what product (in our case vehicle) to instantiate. Concrete subclasses of the factory make that determination. Here is how the *Factory Method* pattern could be used with the `Vehicle` class hierarchy:

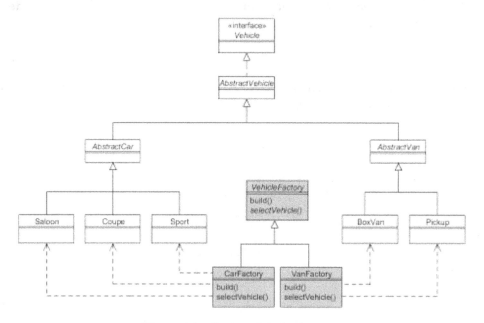

Figure 4.2 : Factory Method pattern

In the above diagram we can see that we have created an abstract `VehicleFactory` class which has two concrete subclasses, `CarFactory` and `VanFactory`. Let us look at how `VehicleFactory` is defined:

vehicle_factory.php

```php
abstract class VehicleFactory {

    const ECONOMICAL   = 'Economical';
    const MIDRANGE     = 'Midrange';
    const POWERFUL     = 'Powerful';

    public function build($driving_style, $colour) {
        $vehicle = $this->selectVehicle($driving_style);
        $vehicle->paint($colour);
        return $vehicle;
    }
```

```
    // This is the "factory method"
    protected abstract function selectVehicle($driving_style);

}
```

VehicleFactory contains the public function build() that takes as arguments the driving style (economical, midrange or powerful) and the colour that the vehicle should be painted. The build() function calls the protected abstract selectVehicle() function, which is the "factory method" after which the pattern is named. The implementation of selectVehicle() is therefore delegated to the subclasses such that each subclass determines the specific type of vehicle to instantiate. The function is protected because we only want subclasses to utilise it – it is not intended to be invoked by clients.

Here is the CarFactory concrete subclass:

car_factory.php

```
class CarFactory extends VehicleFactory {

    protected function selectVehicle($driving_style) {
        switch ($driving_style):
            case VehicleFactory::ECONOMICAL:
                return new Saloon(new StandardEngine(1300));

            case VehicleFactory::MIDRANGE:
                return new Coupe(new StandardEngine(1600));

            default:
                // Must want powerful
                return new Sport(new TurboEngine(2000));
        endswitch;
    }

}
```

As you can see, the selectVehicle() function is implemented such that it works out from the supplied arguments exactly which type of car should be instantiated and returned.

The VanFactory is similar, using the argument to decide which van to instantiate and return:

van_factory.php

```php
class VanFactory extends VehicleFactory {

    protected Vehicle selectVehicle(DrivingStyle style) {
        switch ($driving_style):
            case VehicleFactory::ECONOMICAL:
            case VehicleFactory::MIDRANGE:
                return new Pickup(new StandardEngine(2200));

            default:
                // Must want powerful
                return new BoxVan(new TurboEngine(2500));
        endswitch;
    }

}
```

Client programs instantiate the required factory and call its `build()` function:

```php
// I want an economical car, coloured blue...
$car_factory = new CarFactory();
$car = $car_factory->build(VehicleFactory::ECONOMICAL,
                           Vehicle::BLUE);

// I am a "white van man"...
$van_factory = new VanFactory();
$van = $van_factory->build(VehicleFactory::POWERFUL, Vehicle::WHITE);
```

You should see the following output:

```
Saloon (StandardEngine (1300), Blue)
BoxVan (TurboEngine(2500), White)
```

Using 'static' factory methods

A common and useful variation is to define a `static` factory method. Let's assume we define the following additional constants in the `VehicleFactory` class:

```php
const CAR = 'Car';
const VAN = 'Van';
```

Now we can define the following static `make()` function also in `VehicleFactory` that works out which subclass to instantiate:

```
public static function make($vehicle_type,
                            $drivingStyle style,
                            $colour) {

    if ($vehicle_type == VehicleFactory::CAR):
        $factory = new CarFactory();
    else:
        $factory = new VanFactory();
    endif;

    return $factory->build($driving_style, $colour);
}
```

Using the `static make()` function is very straightforward:

```
// Create a red sports car...
$sporty = VehicleFactory::make(VehicleFactory::CAR,
                               VehicleFactory::POWERFUL,
                               Vehicle::RED);
```

This should give the following output:

```
Sport (TurboEngine (2000), Red)
```

5. Prototype

Type	Creational
Purpose	Specify the kinds of objects to create using a prototypical instance, and create new objects by copying the prototype.

We shall assume in this chapter that instantiating car and van objects is a time-consuming process, and we therefore need to find a way of speeding up instantiation time whenever we need a new vehicle object.

Here is a reminder of the Vehicle class hierarchy:

Figure 5.1 : Vehicle class hierarchy

One approach that may improve instantiation time is to utilise PHP's clone function. We will therefore specify that the Vehicle interface defines the function __clone() with the concrete vehicle classes implementing it. This chapter thus uses a modified version of the Vehicle interface as listed below, where the additional code is indicated in bold:

vehicle.php

```
interface Vehicle {

    const UNPAINTED    = 'Unpainted';
    const BLUE         = 'Blue';
    const BLACK        = 'Black';
    const GREEN        = 'Green';
    const RED          = 'Red';
    const SILVER       = 'Silver';
    const WHITE        = 'White';
    const YELLOW       = 'Yellow';

    public function getEngine();
    public function getColour();
    public function paint($colour);

    public function __clone();

}
```

You need to implement the __clone() function in each of the concrete subclasses:

saloon.php

```
class Saloon extends AbstractCar {

    public function __construct(Engine $engine,
                                $colour = Vehicle::UNPAINTED) {
        parent::__construct($engine, $colour);
    }

    public function __clone() {}

}
```

You should now also add the __clone() function as above to coupe.php, sport.php, boxvan.php and pickup.php. Note that the default operation of __clone() performs a "shallow copy" of the object's properties, but you can override if needed to perform additional steps.

We will now define a VehicleManager class that will create the initial vehicles from which we can obtain clones:

vehicle_manager.php

```
class VehicleManager {

    private $saloon;
    private $coupe;
    private $sport;
    private $boxVan;
    private $pickup;

    public function __construct() {
        // For simplicity all vehicles use same engine type...
        $this->saloon = new Saloon(new StandardEngine(1300));
        $this->coupe = new Coupe(new StandardEngine(1300));
        $this->sport = new Sport(new StandardEngine(1300));
        $this->boxVan = new BoxVan(new StandardEngine(1300));
        $this->pickup = new Pickup(new StandardEngine(1300));
    }

    public function createSaloon() {
        return clone $this->saloon;
    }

    public function createCoupe() {
        return clone $this->coupe;
    }

    public function createSport() {
        return clone $this->sport;
    }

    public function createBoxVan() {
        return clone $this->boxVan;
    }

    public function createPickup() {
        return clone $this->pickup;
    }

}
```

Client programs can use VehicleManager as follows:

```
$vehicle_manager = new VehicleManager();
```

```
$saloon1 = $vehicle_manager->createSaloon();
$saloon2 = $vehicle_manager->createSaloon();
$pickup1 = $vehicle_manager->createPickup();
```

A drawback of `VehicleManager` as coded is that it always instantiates at least one vehicle of each type as part of the construction process. If not all types of vehicles will be needed, a more efficient technique would be to lazy-load by only instantiating the first time each is needed. This is illustrated in the modified version of the class (which we will call `VehicleManagerLazy`) below:

vehicle_manager_lazy.php

```php
class VehicleManagerLazy {

    private $saloon;
    private $coupe;
    private $sport;
    private $boxVan;
    private $pickup;

    public function __construct() {
    }

    public function createSaloon() {
        if (empty($this->$saloon)):
            $this->saloon = new Saloon(new StandardEngine(1300));
        endif;
        return clone $this->saloon;
    }

    public function createCoupe() {
        if (empty($this->coupe)):
            $this->coupe = new Coupe(new StandardEngine(1300));
        endif;
        return clone $this->coupe;
    }

    public function createSport() {
        if (empty($this->sport)):
            $this->sport = new Sport(new StandardEngine(1300));
        endif;
        return clone $this->sport;
    }

    public function createBoxVan() {
        if (empty($this->boxVan)):
            $this->boxVan = new BoxVan(new StandardEngine(1300));
        endif;
        return clone $this->boxVan;
    }
```

```
    public function createPickup() {
        if (empty($this->pickup)):
            $this->pickup = new Pickup(new StandardEngine(1300));
        endif;
        return clone $this->pickup;
    }

}
```

Before a clone is returned, a check is made to ensure that the 'prototype' object exists, and it will be instantiated if necessary. From then on it just clones the previously instantiated object. Client programs can use VehicleManagerLazy in the same way as before:

```
$vehicle_manager = new VehicleManagerLazy();

$saloon1 = $vehicle_manager->createSaloon();
$saloon2 = $vehicle_manager->createSaloon();
$pickup1 = $vehicle_manager->createPickup();
```

6. Singleton

Type	Creational
Purpose	Ensure a class allows only one object to be created, providing a single point of access to it.

The Foobar Motor Company, in common with all vehicle manufacturers, needs to stamp a unique serial number on all vehicles they produce[1]. They want to model this requirement ensuring that there is just one easy place where the next available serial number can be obtained. If we were to have more than one object that generates the next number there is a risk that we could end up with separate numbering sequences, so we need to prevent this.

The *Singleton* pattern provides a way of ensuring that only one instance of a particular class can ever be created. So how can we stop other objects from just invoking new multiple times? There are several ways of accomplishing this, and the "traditional" approach that you may often encounter is to make your constructor private but provide a public static getter function that returns a static instance of the *Singleton* class. This is how it could look:

serial_number_generator.php

```
class SerialNumberGenerator {

    // static variables and functions
    private static $instance;

    public static function getInstance() {
        if (empty(SerialNumberGenerator::$instance)):
            SerialNumberGenerator::$instance =
                        new SerialNumberGenerator();
        endif;
        return SerialNumberGenerator::$instance;
    }
```

---

[1]In the UK this is known as the Vehicle Identification Number (VIN).

```
    // instance variables and functions
    private $count;

    private function __construct() {}

    public function getNextSerial() {
        return ++$this->count;
    }
}
```

Note that the getInstance() function will only instantiate the object once and so the same instance will always be returned. The constructor is private to prevent client programs from calling new, thus enforcing the fact that only one object can ever be created, since they can only go through the getInstance() function. The singleton could be used thus:

```
$serial1 = SerialNumberGenerator::getInstance()->getNextSerial();
$serial2 = SerialNumberGenerator::getInstance()->getNextSerial();
$serial3 = SerialNumberGenerator::getInstance()->getNextSerial();
```

Part III. Structural Patterns

This part describes the seven structural patterns, that is, those that help manage how classes are organised and interrelate.

- *Adapter*: Convert the interface of a class into the interface clients expect, letting classes work together that couldn't otherwise because of incompatible types;

- *Bridge*: Decouple an abstraction from its implementation so that each may vary independently;

- *Composite*: Compose objects into tree structures to represent part-whole hierarchies, letting client objects treat individual objects and compositions uniformly;

- *Decorator*: Attach additional responsibilities to an object dynamically;

- *Façade*: Provide a uniform interface to a set of interfaces in a subsystem, by defining a higher-level interface that makes the subsystem easier to use;

- *Flyweight*: Use sharing to support large numbers of fine-grained objects efficiently;

- *Proxy*: Provide a surrogate or place-holder for another object to control access to it.

7. Adapter

Type	Structural
Purpose	Convert the interface of a class into another interface clients expect. *Adapter* lets classes work together that couldn't otherwise because of incompatible interfaces.

You will recall from the introduction that the Foobar Motor Company makes the engines for their vehicles. Here is a reminder of the Engine hierarchy:

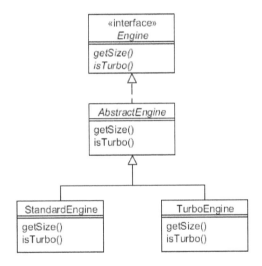

Figure 7.1 : Engine class hierarchy

And here is a reminder of the code of the abstract AbstractEngine class:

abstract_engine.php

```
abstract class AbstractEngine implements Engine {

    private $size;
    private $turbo;
```

```
    public function __construct($size, $turbo) {
        $this->size = $size;
        $this->turbo = $turbo;
    }

    public function getSize() {
        return $this->size;
    }

    public function isTurbo() {
        return $this->turbo;
    }

    public function __toString() {
        return getClass($this) . ' (' . (string)$this->size . ')';
    }

}
```

Let's say our client program takes engines stored in an array and loops through them one at a time displaying the engine size and type:

```
$engines = array(
    new StandardEngine(1300),
    new StandardEngine(1600),
    new TurboEngine(2000)
);
```

In the HTML section

```
<?php foreach ($engines as $engines): ?>
    <p><?php echo $engine; ?></p>
<?php endforeach; ?>
```

Running the above code would result in the following display:

```
StandardEngine (1300)
StandardEngine (1600)
TurboEngine (2000)
```

For this chapter we will assume that in addition to the two concrete subclasses (StandardEngine and TurboEngine) Foobar have decided to use a further engine class named SuperGreenEngine which is made by a different manufacturer.

Because the `SuperGreenEngine` class is provided by a third-party it does not implement our `Engine` interface. Furthermore, Foobar are unable or not allowed to modify the PHP source code, but the following class details are known from the documentation:

- The class does not extend any other;

- The constructor takes one argument for the engine size;

- There is a `getEngineSize()` function that returns the engine size as an integer;

- These types of engines are never turbocharged;

- The `__toString()` function returns a `String` in the format: `SUPER ENGINE nnnn` (where nnnn is the engine size).

We can therefore see that `SuperGreenEngine` uses a different function name to access the engine size and there is no function related to whether it is turbocharged, and that it is not within the `Engine` hierarchy. While it would be possible to add instances of `SuperGreenEngine` to the reporting array you would not have access to the normal functions (`getSize()` and `isTurbo()`) while iterating through it, and the format of the `__toString()` function is different.

The *Adapter* pattern provides an approach to resolve this through the definition of a new class that 'adapts' the class we want to use into the format existing classes require. For our purposes, therefore, we shall create a `SuperGreenEngineAdapter` class:

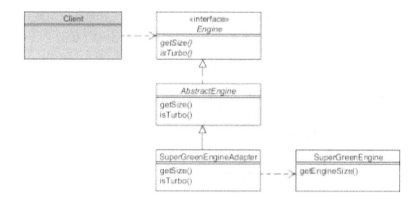

Figure 7.2 : Adapter class hierarchy

The code for the adapter is as follows:

super_green_engine_adapter.php

```php
class SuperGreenEngineAdapter extends AbstractEngine {

    public function __construct(SuperGreenEngine $green_engine) {
        parent::__construct($green_engine->getEngineSize(), false);
    }

}
```

Note the following from the above PHP code:

• We extend the class we are adapting **to**.

• We accept a reference in the constructor to the class we are adapting **from**.

• The constructor obtains the necessary state from the referenced object and passes it to the superclass constructor.

Now we are in a position to include `SuperGreenEngine` objects in our reporting collection (additional code indicated in bold):

```php
// "Adapt" the new engine type...
```

```
$green_engine = new SuperGreenEngine(1200);
$engine_adapter = new SuperGreenEngineAdapter($green_engine);

$engines = array(
    new StandardEngine(1300),
    new StandardEngine(1600),
    new TurboEngine(2000),
    $engine_adapter // adapted engine
);
```

The output should now be:

```
StandardEngine (1300)
StandardEngine (1600)
TurboEngine (2000)
SuperGreenEngineAdapter (1200)
```

Note how the output made use of the `__toString()` function as inherited from `AbstractEngine` rather than that of `SuperGreenEngine`.

Variations for implementing adapters

We were somewhat fortunate in that the design of the `Engine` and `SuperGreenEngine` classes made it easy for the adapter class to do the work inside its constructor. Often however, we need to take a few additional steps inside the code of the adapter class, so here is a general formula to apply:

1. Extend the class you are adapting to (or implement it, if it's an interface);

2. Specify the class you are adapting from in the constructor and store a reference to it in an instance variable;

3. For each function in the class you are extending (or interface you are implementing), override it to delegate to the corresponding function of the class you are adapting from.

Here is a generic example adapter class:

```
class ObjectAdapter extends ClassAdaptingTo {

    private $fromObject;

    public function __construct(FromClass $fromObject) {
        $this->fromObject = $fromObject;
    }

    // Overridden function
    public function functionInToClass() {
        $this->fromObject->functionInFromClass();
    }

}
```

8. Bridge

Type	Structural
Purpose	Decouple an abstraction from its implementation so that each may vary independently.

The Foobar Motor Company manufactures engines for its vehicles. Here is a reminder of the Engine class hierarchy:

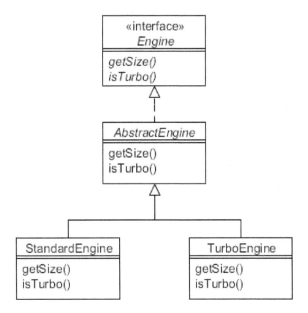

Figure 8.1 : Engine class hierarchy

The implementation of the Engine class as detailed in the introduction, merely stores the engine size (e.g. 1600cc) and whether it is turbocharged. For the purposes of this chapter this class will be enhanced to enable the engine to be started and stopped and for the power to the engine to be increased or decreased.

The modified version of the `Engine` interface and `AbstractEngine` class is listed below with the changes marked in bold:

engine.php

```
interface Engine {
    public function getSize();
    public function isTurbo();

    public function start();
    public function stop();
    public function increasePower();
    public function decreasePower();
}
```

abstract_engine.php

```
abstract class AbstractEngine implements Engine {

    private $size;
    private $turbo;
    private $running;
    private $power;

    public function __construct($size, $turbo) {
        $this->size = $size;
        $this->turbo = $turbo;
        $this->running = false;
        $this->power = 0;
    }

    public function getSize() {
        return $this->size;
    }

    public function isTurbo() {
        return $this->turbo;
    }

    public function start() {
        $this->running = true;
    }

    public function stop() {
        $this->running = false;
        $this->power = 0;
    }

    public function increasePower() {
        if ($this->running and ($this->power < 10)) {
            $this->power++;
        }
```

```
        }

    public function decreasePower() {
        if ($this->running and ($this->power > 0)) {
            $this->power--;
        }
    }

    public function __toString() {
        return getClass($this) . ' (' + $this->size ')';
    }

}
```

Within a vehicle, the driver controls the functions of the engine indirectly by means of various hand and foot controls, such as the ignition switch, accelerator pedal and brake pedal. To retain flexibility, it is important to design the connection between the engine and the controls so that each can vary independently of the other. In other words:

- *A new engine can be designed and plugged into a vehicle without needing any driver controls to be changed; and*

- *New driver controls (for example, to assist disabled drivers) can be designed and plugged into a vehicle without needing the engines to change.*

The *Bridge* pattern addresses this requirement by separating the 'abstraction' from the 'implementation' into two separate but connected hierarchies such that each can vary independently of the other. In our example, the 'abstraction' is the driver controls and the 'implementation' is the engine.

The following diagram shows this relationship:

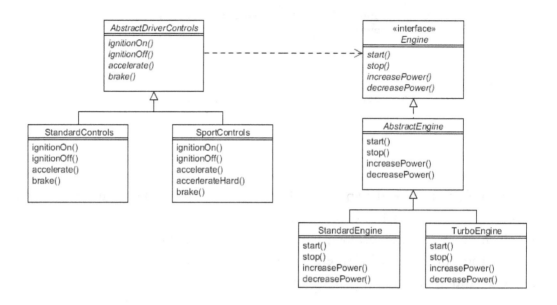

Figure 8.2 : Bridge pattern

As the above figure shows, there is an abstract `AbstractDriverControls` class with two concrete subclasses; `StandardControls` and `SportControls`:

The `AbstractDriverControls` class requires an `Engine` object passed to its constructor and then delegates to the engine for each of its functions:

abstact_driver_controls.php

```php
abstract class AbstractDriverControls {

    private $engine;

    public function __construct(Engine $engine) {
        $this->engine = $engine;
    }

    public function ignitionOn() {
        $this->engine->start();
    }
```

```php
    public function ignitionOff() {
        $this->engine->stop();
    }

    public function accelerate() {
        $this->engine->increasePower();
    }

    public function brake() {
        $this->engine->decreasePower();
    }

}
```

Subclasses of `AbstractDriverControls` can either use the superclass functions as-is or define additional functionality:

The `StandardControls` class uses `AbstractDriverControls` as-is:

standard_controls.php

```php
class StandardControls extends AbstractDriverControls {

    public  function  __construct(Engine $engine) {
        parent::__construct($engine);
    }

    // No extra features

}
```

Whereas the `SportControls` class defines an additional function:

sport_controls.php

```php
class SportControls extends AbstractDriverControls {

    public function __construct(Engine $engine) {
        parent::__construct($engine);
    }

    public function accelerateHard() {
        $this->accelerate();
        $this->accelerate();
    }

}
```

The important point to note from the above is that the additional function is coded in terms of the superclass 'abstraction' and *not* the 'implementation' (engine). So in the above example the `accelerateHard()` function invokes the `accelerate()` function as defined in `AbstractDriverControls`. It is this approach that allows the abstraction and the implementation to vary independently if needed.

Thus we could incorporate a brand-new type of engine without modifying the driver controls classes, provided the engine adheres to the `Engine` contract. Conversely we could develop a new set of driver controls (such as enabling voice activation) without having to modify anything in the `Engine` hierarchy.

Client programs can use the bridge as follows:

```
$engine = new StandardEngine(1300);
$standard_controls = new StandardControls($engine);
$standard_controls->ignitionOn();
$standard_controls->accelerate();
$standard_controls->brake();
$standard_controls->ignitionOff();

// Now use sport controls
$sport_controls = new SportControls($engine);
$sport_controls->ignitionOn();
$sport_controls->accelerate();
$sport_controls->accelerateHard();
$sport_controls->brake();
$sport_controls->ignitionOff();
```

9. Composite

Type	Structural
Purpose	Compose objects into tree structures to represent part-whole hierarchies. *Composite* lets clients treat individual objects and compositions of objects uniformly.

In the Foobar Motor Company workshop they build various items from component parts such as nuts, bolts, panels, etc. Each individual component item has an associated description and unit cost, and when items are assembled into larger items the cost is therefore the sum of its component parts[1].

The *Composite* pattern enables us to treat both individual parts and assemblies of parts as if they are the same, thus enabling them to be processed in a consistent manner, simplifying code. The class hierarchy looks like this:

---

[1] We will ignore the cost of assembly, such as labour costs.

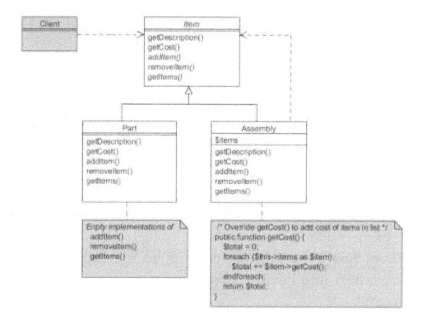

Figure 9.1 : Composite pattern

The abstract `Item` class defines all possible functions for both parts and assemblies of parts:

item.php

```php
abstract class Item {

    private $description;
    private $cost;

    public function __construct($description, $cost) {
        $this->description = $description;
        $this->cost = $cost;
    }

    public function getDescription() {
        return $this->description;
    }

    public function getCost() {
        return $this->cost;
    }

    public abstract function addItem(Item $item);
    public abstract function removeItem(Item $item);
```

```
        public abstract function getItems();

        public function __toString() {
            return $this->description . ' (cost = ' .
                                        $this->getCost() .
                                        ')';
        }


}
```

The above class provides default implementations for getDescription() and getCost(), and defines the abstract functions addItem(), removeItem() and getItems().

Individual parts are modelled using the Part subclass:

part.php

```
    class Part extends Item {

        public function __construct($description, $cost) {
            parent::__construct($description, $cost);
        }

        // Empty implementation for unit parts...
        public function addItem(Item $item) {}
        public function removeItem(Item $item) {}
        public function getItems() {return array();}
    }
```

As you can see, the functions related to managing assemblies of items have empty implementations since a 'part' is the smallest unit possible, and therefore unable to have sub-parts, unlike 'assemblies'.

Assemblies of parts are modelled using the Assembly subclass:

assembly.php

```
    class Assembly extends Item {

        private $items =  array();

        public function __construct($description) {
            parent::__construct($description, 0);
        }

        public function addItem(Item $item) {
```

```
        array_push($this->items, $item);
    }

    public function removeItem(Item $item) {
        unset($this->items[$item]);
    }

    public function getItems() {
        return $this->items;
    }

    // Also have to override getCost() to add cost of items in list
    public function getCost() {
        $total = 0;
        foreach ($this->items as $item) {
            $total += $item->getCost();
        }
        return $total;
    }
}
```

For assemblies, we have implemented the abstract functions to add other
`Item` objects into an internal array. We have also overridden the
`getCost()` function to loop through the array to sum the cost of all
contained items within this assembly.[1]

All types of `Item` objects can now be used in a uniform manner:

```
$nut = new Part('Nut', 5);
$bolt = new Part('Bolt', 9);
$panel = new Part('Panel', 35);

$gizmo = new Assembly('Gizmo');
$gizmo->addItem($panel);
$gizmo->addItem($nut);
$gizmo->addItem($bolt);

$widget = new Assembly('Widget');
$widget.addItem($gizmo);
$widget.addItem($nut);
```

In the above extract, nuts, bolts and panels are defined as individual parts,
a "Gizmo" is assembled from one nut, one bolt and one panel, and a
"Widget" is assembled from one "Gizmo" and another nut.

---

[1] We set the cost to zero when constructing `Assembly` object, since initially it has no component parts until they
are added.

Displaying the objects would result in this:

```
Nut (cost = 5)
Bolt (cost = 9)
Panel (cost = 35)
Gizmo (cost = 49)
Widget (cost = 54)
```

The assemblies have computed the total cost without the client program needing to know how.

10. Decorator

Type	Structural
Purpose	Attach additional responsibilities to an object dynamically. Decorators provide a flexible alternative to subclassing for extending functionality.

You will recall the Foobar Motor Company Vehicle class hierarchy:

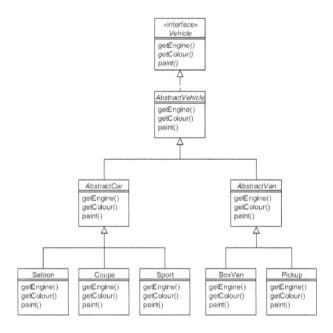

Figure 10.1 : Vehicle class hierarchy

For the purposes of this chapter, we shall add one additional function called getPrice() to the Vehicle interface. We will also modify the __toString() function in AbstractVehicle to include the price. The modified interface and class is shown below with the changes marked in bold:

vehicle.php

```php
interface Vehicle {
    const UNPAINTED   = "Unpainted";
    const BLUE        = "Blue";
    const BLACK       = "Black";
    const GREEN       = "Green";
    const RED         = "Red";
    const SILVER      = "Silver";
    const WHITE       = "White";
    const YELLOW      = "Yellow";

    public function getEngine();
    public function paint($colour);
    public function getColour();
    public function getPrice();
}
```

abstract_vehicle.php

```php
abstract class AbstractVehicle implements Vehicle {

    private $engine;
    private $colour;

    public function __construct(Engine $engine,
                                $color=Vehicle::UNPAINTED) {
        $this->engine = $engine;
        $this->colour = $colour;
    }

    public function getEngine() {
        return $this->engine;
    }

    public  function getColour() {
        return $this->colour;
    }

    public function paint($colour) {
        $this->colour = $colour;
    }

    public function __toString() {
        return getClass($this) . ' (' +
            $this->engine . ',' . $this->colour .
                ', price ' . $this->getPrice() + ')';
    }

}
```

Each of the concrete subclasses implements the `getPrice()` function as appropriate. For example, the `Saloon` class now looks like this (changes in bold):

saloon.php

```
class Saloon extends AbstractCar {

    public function __construct(Engine $engine, $colour) {
        parent::__construct($engine, $colour);
    }

    public function getPrice() {
        return 6000;
    }

}
```

The other subclasses are similarly defined, and the `getPrice()` function returns:

- 6,000 for `Saloon` objects;

- 7,000 for `Coupe` objects;

- 8,000 for `Sport` objects;

- 9,000 for `Pickup` objects;

- 10,000 for `BoxVan` objects.

When a customer buys a vehicle they have the choice of adding any number of optional extras. They can choose from an air-conditioning system, alloy wheels, leather seats, metallic paint, or a satellite-navigation unit. They can choose none at all, or any combination up to all five.

The *Decorator* pattern is designed to facilitate the addition of state and/or behaviour without having to modify the inheritance hierarchy of the classes being added to. This is accomplished by defining a new hierarchy which itself extends the root of the main tree.

This is shown diagrammatically below:

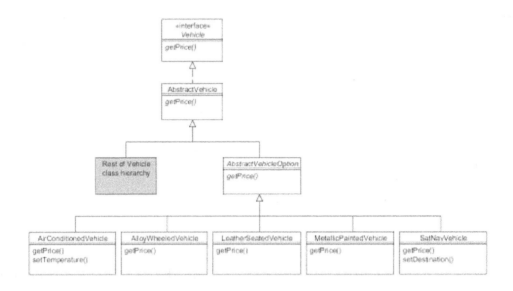

Figure 10.2 : Decorator pattern hierarchy

From the diagram you can see that a new abstract class has been defined called `AbstractVehicleOption` that inherits from `AbstractVehicle`. `AbstractVehicleOption` has five concrete subclasses; one for each option that can be selected.

The `AbstractVehicleOption` class looks like this:

abstract_vehicle_option.php

```php
abstract class AbstractVehicleOption extends AbstractVehicle {

    protected $decoratedVehicle;

    public function __construct(Vehicle $vehicle) {
        parent::__construct($vehicle->getEngine(),
                            $vehicle->getColour());
        $this->decoratedVehicle = $vehicle;
    }

}
```

AbstractVehicleOption is the abstract "decorator" class and it requires a reference to the Vehicle class which is to be decorated.

Each of the option subclasses is straightforward. They all override the getPrice() function to add the price of the option to the price of the object that is being decorated. In the case of the AirConditionedVehicle and SatNavVehicle classes, we have also defined an extra function:

air_conditioned_vehicle.php

```php
class AirConditionedVehicle extends AbstractVehicleOption {

    public function __construct(Vehicle $vehicle) {
        parent::construct($vehicle);
    }

    public function getPrice() {
        return $this->decoratedVehicle->getPrice() + 600;
    }

    public function setTemperature(int value) {
        // code to set the temperature...
    }

}
```

alloy_wheeled_vehicle.php

```php
class AlloyWheeledVehicle extends AbstractVehicleOption {

    public function __construct(Vehicle $vehicle) {
        parent::construct($vehicle);
    }

    public function getPrice() {
        return $this->decoratedVehicle.getPrice() + 250;
    }

}
```

leather_seated_vehicle.php

```php
class LeatherSeatedVehicle extends AbstractVehicleOption {

    public function __construct(Vehicle $vehicle) {
        parent::construct($vehicle);
    }
```

```php
        public function getPrice() {
            return $this->decoratedVehicle->getPrice() + 1200;
        }

    }
```

metallic_painted_vehicle.php

```php
    class MetallicPaintedVehicle extends AbstractVehicleOption {

        public function __construct(Vehicle $vehicle) {
            parent::construct($vehicle);
        }

        public function getPrice() {
            return $this->decoratedVehicle->getPrice() + 750;
        }

    }
```

sat_nav_vehicle.php

```php
    class SatNavVehicle extends AbstractVehicleOption {

        public function __construct(Vehicle $vehicle) {
            parent::construct($vehicle);
        }

        public function getPrice() {
            return $this->decoratedVehicle->getPrice() + 1500;
        }

        public function setDestination($target) {
            // code to set the destination...
        }

    }
```

To use the 'decorators' we initially instantiate the car or van we require and then "wrap" them inside the required decorator or decorators.

Here is an example:

```php
    // Create a blue saloon car...
    $myCar = new Saloon(new StandardEngine(1300));
    $myCar->paint(Vehicle::BLUE);
```

```
// Add air-conditioning to the car...
$myCar = new AirConditionedVehicle($myCar);

// Now add alloy wheels...
$myCar = new AlloyWheeledVehicle($myCar);

// Now add leather seats...
$myCar = new LeatherSeatedVehicle($myCar);

// Now add metallic paint...
$myCar = new MetallicPaintedVehicle($myCar);

// Now add satellite-navigation...
$myCar = new SatNavVehicle($myCar);
```

If you output the $myCar object value at each stage you should see this:

```
Saloon (StandardEngine (1300), Blue, price 6000)
AirConditionedVehicle (StandardEngine (1300), Blue, price 6600)
AlloyWheeledVehicle (StandardEngine (1300), Blue, price 6850)
LeatherSeatedVehicle (StandardEngine (1300), Blue, price 8050)
MetallicPaintedVehicle (StandardEngine (1300), Blue, price 8800)
SatNavVehicle (StandardEngine (1300), Blue, price 10300)
```

The price shown at each stage is the total of the vehicle plus the selected options as each is "added".

The *Decorator* pattern is a good example of preferring object composition over inheritance. Had we attempted to use inheritance for the various vehicle options we would have needed to create many different combinations of subclasses to model each combination of selectable options.

Decorator classes are sometimes called "wrapper" classes, since they serve to "wrap" an object inside another object, usually to add or modify its functionality.

11. Facade

Type	Structural
Purpose	Provide a unified interface to a set of interfaces in a subsystem. *Facade* defines a higher-level interface that makes the subsystem easier to use.

Sometimes you need to perform a series of steps to undertake a particular task, often involving multiple objects. The *Facade* pattern involves the creation of a separate object that simplifies the execution of such steps.

As an example, when the Foobar Motor Company are preparing their vehicles for sale there are a number of steps they have to undertake that utilise various objects. In this chapter we shall assume that the Vehicle interface defines the following additional functions beyond those defined in the introduction.

vehicle.php

```
// Extra functions defined in Vehicle...

public function cleanInterior();
public function cleanExteriorBody();
public function polishWindows();
public function takeForTestDrive();
```

The above functions are implemented in AbstractVehicle as follows:

abstract_vehicle.php

```
public function cleanInterior() {
    return 'Cleaning interior';
}

public function cleanExteriorBody() {
    return 'Cleaning exterior';
}

public function polishWindows() {
    return 'polishing windows';
```

```
    }

    public function takeForTestDrive() {
        return 'taking for test drive';
    }
```

We shall introduce two further simple classes called `Registration` and `Documentation`:

registration.php

```
class Registration {

    private $vehicle;

    public function __construct(Vehicle $vehicle) {
        $this->vehicle = $vehicle;
    }

    public function allocateLicensePlate() {
        // Code omitted...
        Return 'License plate allocated';
    }

    public function allocateVehicleNumber() {
        // Code omitted...
        Return 'Vehicle number allocated';
    }

}
```

documentation.php

```
class Documentation {

    public static function printBrochure(Vehicle $vehicle) {
        // code omitted...
        Return 'Brochure printed';
    }

}
```

To implement the pattern we will create a `VehicleFacade` class that defines a function to prepare the specified vehicle by using the above classes on our behalf:

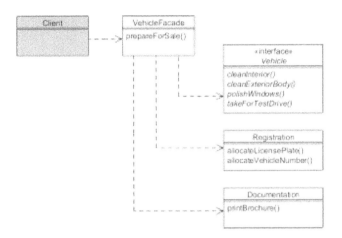

Figure 11.1 : Facade pattern

vehicle_facade.php

```
class VehicleFacade {

    public static function prepareForSale(Vehicle $vehicle) {
        $registration = new Registration($vehicle);
        $registration->allocateVehicleNumber();
        $registration->allocateLicensePlate();

        Documentation::printBrochure($vehicle);

        $vehicle->cleanInterior();
        $vehicle->cleanExteriorBody();
        $vehicle->polishWindows();
        $vehicle->takeForTestDrive();

        return 'vehicle prepared for sale';
    }

}
```

Client programs then only need invoke the `prepareForSale()` function on a `VehicleFacade` instance, and therefore need no knowledge of what needs to be done and what other objects are needed. And if something different is needed in a special circumstance, then the individual functions are still available for calling as required.

12. Flyweight

Type	Structural
Purpose	Use sharing to support large numbers of fine-grained objects efficiently.

Some programs need to create a large number of objects of one particular type, and if those objects happen to have a large amount of state then instantiating lots of them can quickly use up memory. When considering object state, we often note that at least some of it could potentially be shared among a group of objects.

For the Foobar Motor Company, the Engine hierarchy is a case in point:

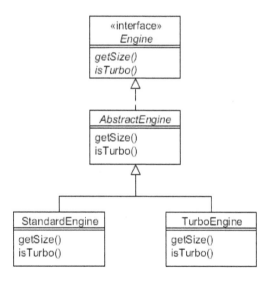

Figure 12.1 : Engine class hierarchy

Our simple implementation of Engine only defines two functions; getSize() and isTurbo(). Let's suppose we instantiate two engines as follows:

```
$engine1 = new StandardEngine(1300);
$engine2 = new StandardEngine(1300);
```

The above would create two separate objects in memory, even though their state is identical. This can be thought of as its *intrinsic state*; i.e. all 1300cc standard engines will be storing *1300* for the engine size and `false` for whether it is turbocharged. Creating hundreds or thousands of these would be wasteful of memory, especially since a more realistic `Engine` class would require many more variables whose values would also be shared.

For the purposes of this chapter another function will be added to the `Engine` interface, called `diagnose()`. This new function will take a `DiagnosticTool` object as its argument, and this argument can be thought of as its *extrinsic state*, since its value is not actually stored in the `Engine` object – it is used purely so that the engine can use it to run a diagnostic check.

The `DiagnosticTool` interface looks like this:

diagnostic_tool.php

```
interface DiagnosticTool {
    public function runDiagnosis($object);
}
```

The `EngineDiagnosticTool` implements the above for running diagnostics on an engine:

engine_diagnostic_tool.php

```
class EngineDiagnosticTool implements DiagnosticTool {

    public function runDiagnosis($engine) {
        return 'Engine diagnosis complete for' . $engine;
    }

}
```

With the above in place we can now add a suitable function to the `Engine` interface:

engine.php

```
interface Engine {

    // Methods having intrinsic state
    public function getSize();
    public function isTurbo();

    // Methods having extrinsic state
    public function diagnose(DiagnosticTool $diagnostic_tool);

}
```

The implementation of this new function in `AbstractEngine` simply issues a call-back to the `DiagnosticTool`:

abstract_engine.php

```
public function diagnose(DiagnosticTool $diagnosticTool) {
    $diagnosticTool->runDiagnosis($this);
}
```

The *Flyweight* pattern allows you to reference a multitude of objects of the same type and having the same state, but only by instantiating the minimum number of actual objects needed. This is typically done by allocating a 'pool' of objects which can be shared, and this is determined by a 'flyweight factory' class. Client programs get access to engines only through the factory:

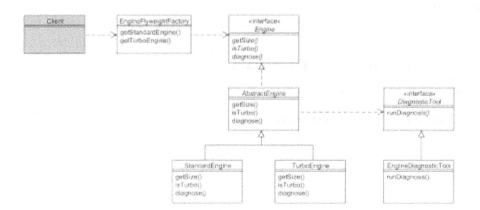

Figure 12.2 : Flyweight pattern

The EngineFlyweightFactory **class looks like this:**

engine_flyweight_factory.php

```php
class EngineFlyweightFactory {

    private $standardEnginePool = array();
    private $turboEnginePool = array();

    public function getStandardEngine($size) {
        if (isset($this->standardEnginePool[$size])):
            $engine = $this->standardEnginePool[$size];
        else:
            $engine = new StandardEngine($size);
            $this->standardEnginePool[$size] = $engine;
        endif;
        return $engine;
    }

    public Engine getTurboEngine(int size) {
        if (isset($this->turboEnginePool[$size])):
            $engine = $this->turboEnginePool[$size];
        else:
            $engine = new TurboEngine($size);
            $this-> turboEnginePool[$size] = $engine;
        endif;
        return $engine;
    }

}
```

This class utilises two arrays (one for standard engines and the other for turbo engines). Each time an engine of a particular type and size is requested, if a similar one has already been created it is returned rather than instantiating a new one.

Client programs use the factory like this:

```
// Create the flyweight factory...
$factory = new EngineFlyweightFactory();

// Create the diagnostic tool
$tool = new EngineDiagnosticTool();

// Get the flyweights and run diagnostics on them
$standard1 = $factory->getStandardEngine(1300);
$standard1->diagnose($tool);

$standard2 = $factory->getStandardEngine(1300);
$standard2->diagnose($tool);

$standard3 = $factory->getStandardEngine(1300);
$standard3->diagnose($tool);

$standard4 = $factory->getStandardEngine(1600);
$standard4->diagnose($tool);

$standard5 = $factory->getStandardEngine(1600);
$standard5->diagnose($tool);

// Show that objects are shared (in HTML output section)
<?php echo spl_object_hash($standard1); ?>
<?php echo spl_object_hash($standard2); ?>
<?php echo spl_object_hash($standard3); ?>
<?php echo spl_object_hash($standard4); ?>
<?php echo spl_object_hash($standard5); ?>
```

In the above, the variables $standard1, $standard2 and $standard3 all reference the same Engine object (since they all 1300cc standard engines). Likewise, $standard4 references the same object as $standard5. Of course, whether it is worth running the diagnostics multiple times on the same objects is arguable depending upon the circumstances!

If the arguments passed to the extrinsic function (DiagnosticTool in our example) need to be stored, this should be done in the client program.

13. Proxy

Type	Structural
Purpose	Provide a surrogate or place-holder for another object to control access to it.

Some functions can be time-consuming, such as those that load complex graphics or need network connections. In these instances, the *Proxy* pattern provides a 'stand-in' object until such time that the time-consuming resource is complete, allowing the rest of your application to load.

In the chapter discussing the *Flyweight* pattern, the `Engine` hierarchy was enhanced to define the additional function `diagnose()`. As you saw, the implementation of `runDiagnosis()` in `EngineDiagnosticTool` is potentialy slow, so we might consider making this run through a proxy object. The proxy could then invoke the diagnosis as a separate thread.

Here is a reminder of the `Engine` hierarchy with the additional function:

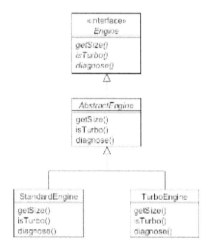

Figure 13.1 : Engine class hierarchy

The *Proxy* pattern involves creating a class that implements the same interface that we are standing-in for, in our case `Engine`. The proxy then forwards requests to the "real" object which it stores internally. Clients just access the proxy:

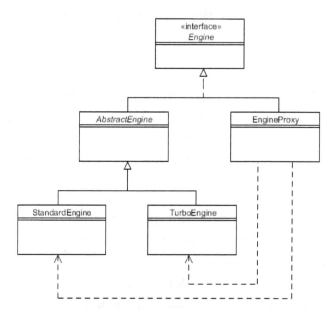

Figure 13.2 : Proxy pattern

Here is the code for the `EngineProxy` class:

engine_proxy.php

```
class EngineProxy implements Engine {

    private $engine;

    public function __construct($size, $turbo) {
        if ($turbo == true):
            $this->engine = new TurboEngine($size);
        else:
            $this->engine = new StandardEngine($size);
        endif;
    }

    public function getSize() {
        return $this->engine->getSize();
```

```
        }

        public function isTurbo() {
            return $this->engine->isTurbo();
        }

        // This function is potentially time-consuming...
        public function diagnose(DiagnosticTool $diagnostic_tool) {
            // This section could be setup as a separate thread
            // if you use the PECL extensions to PHP
            return $diagnostic_tool->runDiagnosis($this->engine);
        }

    }
```

The constructor creates either a StandardEngine or TurboEngine object and stores a reference to it as an instance variable. Calls to getSize() and isTurbo() simply forward to the referenced engine object. Calls to diagnose() will invoke a separate thread to run the actual diagnosis. This can be useful if you cannot modify the original source for some reason.

This leaves the question of how you can 'force' client programs to use the proxy class instead of the normal class, and this is where a 'factory' class may be useful: see Simple Factory (Chapter 26).

Part IV. Behavioural Patterns

This part describes the eleven behavioural patterns, that is, those that help manage what the classes actually do.

- *Chain of Responsibility*: Avoid coupling the sender of a request to its receiver by giving more than one object the chance to handle the request;

- *Command*: Encapsulate a request as an object, thereby letting you parameterise clients with different requests;

- *Interpreter*: Define the representation of a language's grammar;

- *Iterator*: Provide a way to access the elements of an aggregate object sequentially without exposing its underlying representation;

- *Mediator*: Define an object that encapsulates how a set of objects interact;

- *Memento*: Capture and externalise an object's state so that it can be restored to that state later;

- *Observer*: Define a one-to-many dependency between objects so that when one object changes its state, all of its dependents are notified and updated automatically;

- *State*: Allow an object to alter its behaviour when its internal state changes, as if it were a different class;

- *Strategy*: Allow clients to change the algorithm that an object uses to perform a function;

- *Template Method*: Define the skeleton of an algorithm in a function, deferring some steps to subclasses;

- *Visitor.* Simulate the addition of a function to a class without needing to actually change the class.

14. Chain of Responsibility

Type	Behavioural
Purpose	Avoid coupling the sender of a request to its receiver by giving more than one object a chance to handle the request. Chain the receiving objects and pass the request along the chain until an object handles it.

The Foobar Motor Company receives many emails each day, including servicing requests, sales enquiries, complaints, and of course the inevitable spam. Rather than employ someone specifically to sort through each email to determine which department it should be forwarded to, our task is to try and automate this by analysing the text in each email and making a "best guess".

In our simplified example, we will search the text of the email for a number of keywords and depending upon what we find will process accordingly. Here are the words we will search for and how they should be handled:

Keywords	Forward to
"viagra", "pills", "medicines"	Spam handler
"buy", "purchase"	Sales department
"service", "repair"	Servicing department
"complain", "bad"	Manager
Anything else...	General enquiries

Note that only one object needs to handle the request, so if a particular email contains both "purchase" and "repair" it will be forwarded to the sales department only. The sequence in which to check the keywords is whatever seems most sensible for the application; so here we are trying to filter out spam before it reaches any other department.

Now it would be possible, of course, to just have a series of if...else... statements when checking for the keywords, but that would not be very object-oriented. The *Chain of Responsibility* pattern instead allows us to define separate 'handler' objects that all conform to an EmailHandler interface. This enables us to keep each handler independent and loosely-coupled.

The following diagram shows the pattern:

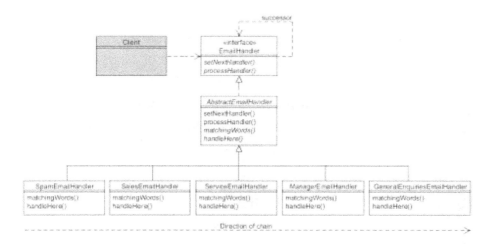

Figure 14.1 : Chain of Responsibility pattern

EmailHandler is the interface at the top of the hierarchy:

email_handler.php

```
interface EmailHandler {
    public function setNextHandler(EmailHandler $handler);
    public function processHandler($email);
}
```

The setNextHandler() function takes another EmailHandler object as its argument which represents the handler to call if the current object is unable to handle the email.

The `processHandler()` function takes the email text as its argument and determines if it is able to handle it (i.e. if it contains one of the keywords we are interested in). If the active object can handle the email it does so, otherwise it just forwards to the next in the chain.

The `AbstractEmailHandler` class implements the `EmailHandler` interface to provide useful default functionality:

abstract_email_handler.php

```php
abstract class AbstractEmailHandler implements EmailHandler {

    private $nextHandler;

    public function setNextHandler(EmailHandler $nextHandler) {
        $this->nextHandler = $nextHandler;
    }

    public function processHandler($email) {
        $wordFound = false;

        // If no words to match against then this object can handle
        if (count(matchingWords()) == 0):
            $wordFound = true;

        else:
            // Look for any of the matching words
            foreach ($this->matchingWords() as $word):
                if (strpos($email, $word) !== false):
                    $wordFound = true;
                    break;
                endif;
            endforeach;
        endif;

        // Can we handle email in this object?
        if ($wordFound == true):
            return $this->handleHere($email);
        else:
            // Unable to handle here so forward to next in chain
            return $this->nextHandler->processHandler($email);
        endif;
    }

    protected abstract function matchingWords();
    protected abstract function handleHere($email);

}
```

The function `setNextHandler()` simply stores the argument in an instance variable; the decision making process is made in `processHandler()`. This has been written to utilise two `abstract` helper functions that must be implemented by concrete subclasses:

- `matchingWords()` will return an array of words that this handler is interested in;

- `handleHere()` is only called if this object can actually handle the email and contains whatever code is required to handle it.

The concrete subclasses are straightforward:

spam_email_handler.php

```php
class SpamEmailHandler extends AbstractEmailHandler {

    protected function matchingWords() {
        return array('viagra', 'pills', 'medicines');
    }

    protected function handleHere($email) {
        return 'This is a spam email';
    }

}
```

sales_email_handler.php

```php
class SalesEmailHandler extends AbstractEmailHandler {

    protected function matchingWords() {
        return array('buy', 'purchase');
    }

    protected function handleHere($email) {
        return 'Email handled by sales department';
    }

}
```

service_email_handler.php

```
class ServiceEmailHandler extends AbstractEmailHandler {

    protected function matchingWords() {
        return array('service', 'repair');
    }

    protected function handleHere($email) {
        return 'Email handled by service department';
    }

}
```

manager_email_handler.php

```
class ManagerEmailHandler extends AbstractEmailHandler {

    protected function matchingWords() {
        return array('complain', 'bad');
    }

    protected function handleHere($email) {
        return 'Email handled by manager';
    }

}
```

general_enquiries_email_handler.php

```
class GeneralEnquiriesEmailHandler extends AbstractEmailHandler {

    protected function matchingWords() {
        return array();  // match anything
    }

    protected function handleHere($email) {
        return 'Email handled by general enquiries;
    }

}
```

We now need to define the sequence in which the handlers are called. For this example, the following static function has been added to AbstractEmailHandler:

abstract_email_handler.php

```
public static function handle($email) {
```

```
    // Create the handler objects...
    $spam = new SpamEmailHandler();
    $sales = new SalesEmailHandler();
    $service = new ServiceEmailHandler();
    $manager = new ManagerEmailHandler();
    $general = new GeneralEnquiriesEmailHandler();

    // Chain them together...
    $spam->setNextHandler($sales);
    $sales->setNextHandler($service);
    $service->setNextHandler($manager);
    $manager->setNextHandler($general);

    // Start the ball rolling...
    return $spam->processHandler($email);
}
```

Putting a message through the handlers is now as simple as this:

```
$mail = "I need my car repaired.";
AbstractEmailHandler::handle($email);
```

This should produce the following output:

```
Email handled by service department.
```

15. Command

Type	Behavioural
Purpose	Encapsulate a request as an object, thereby letting you parameterise clients with different requests, queue or log requests, and support undoable operations.

The vehicles made by the Foobar Motor Company each have an installed radio; this is modelled by the following `Radio` class:

radio.php

```php
class Radio {

    const MIN_VOLUME = 0;
    const MAX_VOLUME = 10;
    const DEFAULT_VOLUME = 5;

    private $on;
    private $volume;

    public function __construct() {
        $this->on = false;
        $this->volume = Radio::DEFAULT_VOLUME;
    }

    public function isOn() {
        return $this->on;
    }

    public function getVolume() {
        return $this->volume;
    }

    public function on() {
        $this->on = true;
    }

    public function off() {
        $this->on = false;
    }

    public function volumeUp() {
        if ($this->isOn()):
            if ($this->getVolume() < Radio:MAX_VOLUME):
                $this->volume++;
            endif;
```

```
            endif;
        }

    public function volumeDown() {
        if ($this->isOn()):
            if ($this->getVolume() > Radio::MIN_VOLUME):
                $this->volume--;
            endif;
        endif;
    }


}
```

As you can see, the class enables the radio to be switched on and off, and provided it is switched on will enable the volume to be increased or decreased one level at a time, within the range 1 to 10[1].

Some of the vehicles also have electrically operated windows with simple up & down buttons, as modelled by the following ElectricWindow class[2].

electric_window.php

```
class ElectricWindow {

    private $open;

    public function __construct() {
        $this->open = false;
    }

    public function isOpen() {
        return $this->open;
    }

    public function isClosed() {
        return (! $this->open);
    }

    public function openWindow() {
        if ($this->isClosed()):
            $this->open = true;
        endif;
    }
```

_____

[1]The code to set the station frequency has been omitted.
[2]For simplicity the windows can only be either fully open or fully closed.

```
        public function closeWindow() {
            if ($this->isOpen()):
                $this->open = false;
            endif;
        }

    }
```

Each of the devices (the radio and the electric window) has separate controls, typically buttons, to manage their state. But suppose the Foobar Motor Company now wishes to introduce speech recognition to their top-of-the-range vehicles and have them perform as follows:

- *If the speech-recognition system is in "radio" mode, then if it hears the word "up" or "down" it adjusts the radio volume; or*

- *If the speech-recognition system is in "window" mode, then if it hears the word "up" or "down" it closes or opens the driver's door window.*

We therefore need the speech-recognition system to be able to handle either `Radio` objects or `ElectricWindow` objects, which are of course in completely separate hierarchies. We might also want it to handle other devices in the future, such as the vehicle's speed or the gearbox (e.g. upon hearing "up" it would increase the speed by 1mph or it would change to the next higher gear). For good object-oriented design we need to isolate the speech-recognition from the devices it controls, so it can cope with any device without directly knowing what they are.

The *Command* patterns allows us to uncouple an object making a request from the object that receives the request and performs the action, by means of a "middle-man" object known as a "command object".

In its simplest form, this requires us to create an interface (which we shall call `Command`) with one function:

command.php

```
    public interface Command {
        public function execute();
    }
```

We now need to create implementing classes for each action that we wish to take[1]. For example, to turn up the volume of the radio we can create a `VolumeUpCommand` class:

volume_up_command.php

```
class VolumeUpCommand implements Command {

    private $radio;

    public function __construct(Radio $radio) {
        $this->radio = $radio;
    }

    public function execute() {
        $this->radio->volumeUp();
    }

}
```

The class simply takes a reference to a `Radio` object in its constructor and invokes its `volumeUp()` function whenever `execute()` is called.

We likewise need to create a `VolumeDownCommand` class for when the volume is to be reduced:

volume_down_command.php

```
class VolumeDownCommand implements Command {

    private $radio;

    public function __construct(Radio $radio) {
        $this->radio = $radio;
    }

    public function execute() {
        $this->radio->volumeDown();
    }

}
```

---

[1] The *Command* pattern is sometimes known as the *Action* pattern.

Controlling an electric window's up and down movement is just as easy: this time we create classes implementing Command passing in a reference to an ElectricWindow object:

window_up_command.php

```php
class WindowUpCommand implements Command {

    private $electricWindow;

    public function __construct(ElectricWindow $electricWindow) {
        $this->electricWindow = $electricWindow;
    }

    public function execute() {
        $this->electricWindow->closeWindow();
    }
}
```

window_down_command.php

```php
class WindowDownCommand implements Command {

    private $electricWindow;

    public function __construct(ElectricWindow $electricWindow) {
        $this->electric_window = $electric_window;
    }

    public function execute() {
        $this->electricWindow->openWindow();
    }

}
```

We will now define a SpeechRecogniser class that only knows about Command objects – it knows nothing about radios or electric windows.

speech_recogniser.php

```php
class SpeechRecogniser {

    private $upCommand, $downCommand;

    public function setCommands(Command $upCommand,
                                Command $downCommand) {
        $this->upCommand = $upCommand;
        $this->downCommand = $downCommand;
```

```
    }

    public function hearUpSpoken() {
        $this->upCommand->execute();
    }

    public void hearDownSpoken() {
        $this->downCommand->execute();
    }
}
```

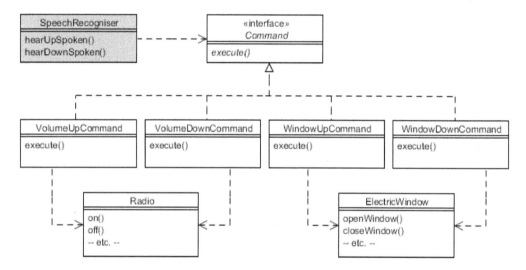

We can view what we have created diagrammatically as follows:

Figure 15.1 : Command pattern

Client programs can now create `Radio` and `ElectricWindow` instances, along with their respective `Command` instances. The command instances are then passed to the `SpeechRecogniser` object so it knows what to do.

We will first create a `Radio` and an `ElectricWindow` and their respective commands:

```
// Create a radio and its up/down command objects
```

```
$radio = new Radio();
$radio->on();
$volumeUpCommand = new VolumeUpCommand($radio);
$volumeDownCommand = new VolumeDownCommand($radio);

// Create an electric window and its up/down command objects
$window = new ElectricWindow();
$windowUpCommand = new WindowUpCommand($window);
$windowDownCommand = new WindowDownCommand($window);
```

Now create a single `SpeechRecogniser` object and set it to control the radio:

```
// Create a speech recognition object
$speechRecogniser = new SpeechRecogniser();

// Control the radio
$speechRecogniser->setCommands($volumeUpCommand, $volumeDownCommand);
$speechRecogniser->hearUpSpoken();
$speechRecogniser->hearDownSpoken();
```

Now set the *same* `SpeechRecogniser` object to control the window instead:

```
// Control the electric window
$speechRecogniser->setCommands($windowUpCommand, $windowDownCommand);
$speechRecogniser->hearDownSpoken();
$speechRecogniser->hearUpSpoken();
```

Typical uses of the Command Pattern

One of the most frequent uses of the *Command* pattern is in UI toolkits. These provide pre-built components like graphical buttons and menu items that cannot possibly know what needs to be done when clicked, because that is always specific to your application. Graphical applications often define both a menubar item and a toolbar icon that perform the same action (e.g. the `File` | `Open` menu item, and an 'Open' icon on a toolbar), where a single command object handles the action that is taken when either is selected.

Another common aspect of graphical applications is the provision of an "undo" mechanism. The *Command* pattern is used to accomplish this too;

using the example in this chapter, we would add a function to the Command interface like this:

command.php

```
interface Command {
    public function execute();
    public function undo();
}
```

Implementing classes then provide the code for the additional function to reverse the last action, as in this example for the VolumeUpCommand class:

volume_up_command.php

```
class VolumeUpCommand implements Command {

    private $radio;

    public function __construct(Radio $radio) {
        $this->radio = $radio;
    }

    public function execute() {
        $this->radio->volumeUp();
    }

    public function undo() {
        $this->radio->volumeDown();
    }

}
```

Most applications would be slightly more involved than the above example, in that you would need to store the state of the object prior to performing the code in the execute() function, enabling you to restore that state when undo() is called.

16. Interpreter

Type	Behavioural
Purpose	Given a language, define a representation for its grammar along with an interpreter that uses the representation to interpret sentences in the language.

The satellite-navigation systems fitted to some of the Foobar Motor Company's vehicles have a special feature that enables the user to enter a number of cities and let it calculate the most northerly, southerly, westerly or easterly, depending on which command string is entered. A sample command might look like this:

```
london edinburgh manchester southerly
```

The above would result in "London" being returned, being the most southerly of the three entered cities. You can even enter the command string like this:

```
london edinburgh manchester southerly aberdeen westerly
```

This would first determine that London was the most southerly and then use that result (London) and compare it to Aberdeen to tell you which of those two is the most westerly[1]. Any number of cities can be entered before each of the directional commands of "northerly", "southerly", "westerly" and "easterly".

You can think of the above command string consisting of the city names and directional keywords as forming a simple "language" that needs to be

---

[1] It's Aberdeen.

interpreted by the satellite-navigation software. The *Interpreter* pattern is an approach that helps to decipher these kinds of relatively simple languages.

Before looking at the pattern itself, we shall create a class named `City` which models the essential points of interest for our example, which is just the name of the city and its latitude and longitude:

city.php

```php
class City {

    private $name, $latitude, $longitude;

    public function __construct($name, $latitude, $longitude) {
        $this->name = $name;
        $this->latitude = $latitude;
        $this->longitude = $longitude;
    }

    public function getName() {
        return $this->name;
    }

    public function getLatitude() {
        return $this->latitude;
    }

    public function getLongitude() {
        return $this->longitude;
    }

    public function __toString() {
        return $this->getName();
    }

}
```

Note that for the latitude positive values represent North and negative values represent South. Similarly, a positive longitude represents East and negative values West. The example in this chapter only includes a small number of UK cities which are all Northern latitude and Western longitude, although any city should work should you wish to use your own.

The classes to interpret the language are structured as follows:

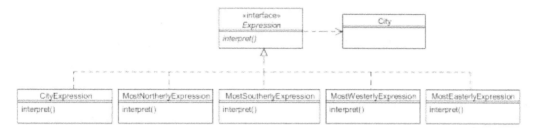

Figure 16.1 : Interpreter pattern

The *Interpreter* pattern resembles the *Composite* pattern in that it comprises an interface (or abstract class) with two types of concrete subclass; one type that represents the individual elements and the other type that represents repeating elements. We create one subclass to handle each type of element in the language.

The Expression interface is very simple, merely declaring an interpret() function that returns a City object:

expression.php

```
interface Expression {
    public function interpret();
}
```

The first concrete subclass we will look at is CityExpression, an instance of which will be created for each city name it recognises in the command string. All this class needs to do is store a reference to a City object and return it when interpret() is invoked:

```
class CityExpression implements Expression {

    private $city;

    public function __construct(City $city) {
        $this->city = $city;
    }

    public function interpret() {
        return $this->city;
    }
}
```

The classes to handle each of the commands (e.g. "northerly") are slightly more involved:

most_northerly_expression.php

```
class MostNortherlyExpression implements Expression {

    private $expressions = array();

    public function __construct(array $expressions) {
        $this->expressions = $expressions;
    }

    public function interpret() {
        $resultingCity = new City("Nowhere", -999.9, -999.9);
        for ($this->expressions as $currentExpression) {
            $currentCity = $currentExpression->interpret();
            if ($currentCity->getLatitude() >
                        $resultingCity->getLatitude()) {
                $resultingCity = $currentCity;
            }
        }
        return $resultingCity;
    }

}
```

The list of `Expression` objects passed to the constructor will be of the `CityExpression` type. The `interpret()` function loops through each of these to determine the most northerly, by comparing their latitude values.

The `MostSoutherlyExpression` class is very similar, merely changing the comparison:

most_southerly_expression.php

```
MostSoutherlyExpression implements Expression {

    private $expressions = array();

    public function __construct(array $expressions) {
        $this->expressions = $expressions;
    }

    public function interpret() {
        $resultingCity = new City("Nowhere", 999.9, 999.9);
        for ($this->expressions as $currentExpression) {
```

```
            $currentCity = $currentExpression->interpret();
            if ($currentCity->getLatitude() <
                            $resultingCity->getLatitude()) {
                $resultingCity = $currentCity;
            }
        }
        return $resultingCity;
    }
}
```

Likewise the `MostWesterlyExpression` and `MostEasterlyExpression` classes compute and return the appropriate `City`:

most_westerly_expression.php

```
class MostWesterlyExpression implements Expression {

    private $expressions = array();

    public function __construct(array $expressions) {
        $this->expressions = $expressions;
    }

    public function interpret() {
        $resultingCity = new City("Nowhere", 999.9, 999.9);
        for ($this->expressions as $currentExpression) {
            $currentCity = $currentExpression->interpret();
            if ($currentCity->getLongitude() <
                            $resultingCity->getLongitude()) {
                $resultingCity = $currentCity;
            }
        }
        return $resultingCity;
    }
}
```

most_easterly_expression.php

```
class MostEasterlyExpression implements Expression {

    private $expressions = array();

    public function __construct(array $expressions) {
        $this->expressions = $expressions;
    }

    public function interpret() {
        $resultingCity = new City("Nowhere", -999.9, -999.9);
        for ($this->expressions as $currentExpression) {
            $currentCity = $currentExpression->interpret();
            if ($currentCity->getLongitude() >
```

```
                               $resultingCity->getLongitude()) {
                    $resultingCity = $currentCity;
                }
            }
        return $resultingCity;
        }
    }
```

While the *Interpreter* pattern does not in itself cover the parsing of an expression, in practice we need to define a class to go through the command string (such as "london edinburgh manchester southerly") and create the appropriate `Expression` classes as we go along. These `Expression` classes are placed into a "syntax tree" which is normally implemented using a LIFO[1] stack. We shall therefore define a `DirectionalEvaluator` class to do this parsing, and set-up a small sample of UK cities:

directional_evaluator.php

```
class DirectionalEvaluator {

    private $cities = array();

    public DirectionalEvaluator() {
        $this->cities["aberdeen"] =
                new City("Aberdeen", 57.15, -2.15);
        $this->cities["belfast"] =
                new City("Belfast", 54.62, -5.93);
        $this->cities["birmingham"] =
                new City("Birmingham", 52.42, -1.92);
        $this->cities["dublin"] =
                new City("Dublin", 53.33, -6.25);
        $this->cities["edinburgh"] =
                new City("Edinburgh", 55.92, -3.02);
        $this->cities["glasgow] =
                new City("Glasgow", 55.83, -4.25);
        $this->cities["london"] =
                new City("London", 51.53, -0.08);
        $this->cities["liverpool"] =
                new City("Liverpool", 53.42, -3.0);
        $this->cities["manchester"] =
                new City("Manchester", 53.5, -2.25);
        $this->cities["southampton"] =
                new City("Southampton", 50.9, -1.38);
    }
```

---

[1]Last In First Out.

```php
    public function evaluate($route) {
        // Define the syntax tree
        $expressionStack = array();

        // Parse each token in route string
        $route_array = explode(' ', $route);
        foreach ($route_array as $token):
            // Is token a recognised city?
            if (isset($this->cities[$token])):
                array_push($expressionStack,
                        new CityExpression($this->city[$token]));

            // Is token to find most northerly?
            elseif ($token == "northerly"):
                array_push($expressionStack,
                    new MostNortherlyExpression
                        ($this->loadExpressions($expressionStack)));

            // Is token to find most southerly?
            elseif ($token == "southerly"):
                array_push($expressionStack,
                    new MostSoutherlyExpression
                        ($this->loadExpressions($expressionStack)));

            // Is token to find most westerly?
            elseif ($token == "westerly"):
                array_push($expressionStack,
                    new MostWesterlyExpression
                        ($this->loadExpressions($expressionStack)));

            // Is token to find most easterly?
            elseif ($token =="easterly"):
                array_push($expressionStack,
                    new MostEasterlyExpression
                        ($this->loadExpressions($expressionStack)));
            endif;
        endforeach;

        // Resulting value
        return array_pop($expressionStack)->interpret();
    }

    // Note: parameter must be passed by reference
    private function loadExpressions(array &$expressionStack) {
        $expressions = array();
        while(! empty($expressionStack)):
            array_push($expressions, array_pop($expressionStack));
        endwhile;
        return $expressions;
    }

}
```

Within the `evaluate()` function, when the parser detects a directional command (such as "northerly") it removes the cities on the stack and passes them along with the command back to the stack.

> Note that the use above of `if...else...` statements has been used simply so that the chapter concentrates on the *Interpreter* pattern. A better approach would be to use a separate pattern to handle each token such as that defined in *Chain of Responsibility*.

Now all that remains is for our client programs to utilise the `DirectionalEvaluator` passing the command to interpret:

```
// Create the evaluator
$evaluator = new DirectionalEvaluator();

// This should return "London"...
$evaluator->evaluate("london edinburgh manchester southerly"));

// This should return "Aberdeen"...
$evaluator->evaluate("london edinburgh manchester southerly aberdeen
                                                        westerly"));
```

17. Iterator

Type	Behavioural
Purpose	Provide a way to access the elements of an aggregate object sequentially without exposing its underlying representation.

"Iteration" describes the process of going through a collection of like items one at a time. This is generally accomplished in PHP by using `foreach` or `while`.

The Foobar Motor Company wants to produce a brochure listing their range of vehicles for sale in two separate classes, one for cars and the other for vans.

For the `CarRange` class use is made of PHP's `Iterator` interface which requires the implementation of a small number of functions, as below:

car_range.php

```
class CarRange implements Iterator {

    private $cars = array();
    private $index = 0;

    public function __construct() {
        $this->cars[0] = new Saloon(new StandardEngine(1300));
        $this->cars[1] = new Saloon(new StandardEngine(1600));
        $this->cars[2] = new Coupe(new StandardEngine(2000));
        $this->cars[3] = new Sport(new TurboEngine(2500));
    }

    // Move the iterator back to the beginning
    public function rewind() {
        $this->index = 0;
    }

    // Return true if there is a current element
    public function valid() {
        return isset($this->cars[$this->index]);
    }

    // Return the current element
    public function current() {
```

```
        return $this->cars[$this->index];
    }

    // Return the current index
    public function key() {
        return $this->index;
    }

    // Point to next element
    public function next() {
        $this->index++;
    }

}
```

You can loop through any object that implements Iterator using a standard foreach construct:

```
$carRange = new CarRange();

foreach ($carRange as $car):
    // Do something with $car...
endforeach;
```

For the VanRange class use is instead made of the IteratorAggregate interface, which requires only one function to be defined that returns an Iterator object. Another PHP supplied class, ArrayIterator, converts an array into an iterator for you:

van_range.php

```
class VanRange implements IteratorAggregate {

    private $vans = array();

    public function __construct() {
        $this->vans[0] = new BoxVan(new StandardEngine(1600));
        $this->vans[1] = new BoxVan(new StandardEngine(2000));
        $this->vans[2] = new Pickup(new TurboEngine(2200));
    }

    public function getIterator() {
        return new ArrayIterator($this->vans);
    }

}
```

The `VanRange` objects also can be processed using a `foreach` construct identically to `CarRange`. Clearly, the `VanRange` implementation is easier, but occasionally you may need to have finer control over the iteration (such as restarting the loop from the beginning) in which case using `Iterator` would enable this. PHP contains several other useful iteration classes, such as `RecursiveArrayIterator`, `CachingIterator`, `RegexIterator`, etc. Refer to the PHP documentation for more details.

18. Mediator

Type	Behavioural
Purpose	Define an object that encapsulates how a set of objects interact. *Mediator* promotes loose coupling by keeping objects from referring to each other explicitly, and it lets you vary their interaction independently.

The Foobar Motor Company is looking to the future when vehicles can drive themselves. This, of course, would entail the various components (ignition, gearbox, accelerator and brakes, etc.) being controlled together and interacting in various ways. For example:

- *Until the ignition is switched on, the gearbox, accelerator and brakes do not operate (we will assume the parking brake is in effect);*

- *When accelerating, the brakes should be disabled;*

- *When braking the accelerator should be disabled;*

- *The appropriate gear should be engaged dependent upon the speed of the vehicle.*

And all this should happen automatically so the driver can just enjoy the view! (We will assume the vehicle can sense its position so as to avoid crashes, etc.).

We will naturally create PHP classes to model the individual components, so there will be an `Ignition` class, a `Gearbox` class, an `Accelerator` class and a `Brake` class. But we can also see that there are some complex interactions between them, and yet one of our core object-oriented design principles is to keep classes loosely-coupled.

The *Mediator* pattern helps to solve this through the definition of a separate class (the mediator) that knows about the individual component classes and takes responsibility for managing their interaction. The component classes also each know about the mediator class, but this is the only coupling they have. For our example, we will call the mediator class `EngineManagementSystem`.

We can see the connections diagrammatically below:

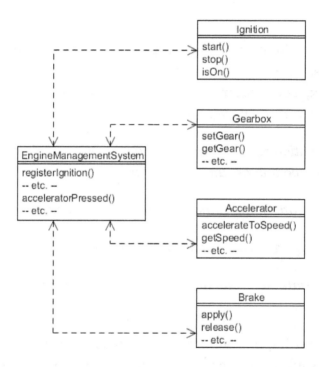

Figure 18.1 : Mediator pattern

The two-way communication is achieved via each of the component classes' constructors, in that they each accept a reference to the mediator object (so they can send messages to it) and register themselves with the mediator (so they can receive messages from it). But each component class has no knowledge of any other component class; they only know about the mediator.

We can see this by looking at the `Ignition` class:

ignition.php

```php
class Ignition {

    private $mediator;
    private $on;

    // Constructor accepts mediator as an argument
    public function __construct(EngineManagementSystem $mediator) {
        $this->mediator = $mediator;
        $this->on = false;

        // Register back with the mediator...
        $this->mediator->registerIgnition($this);
    }

    public function start() {
        $this->on = true;
        $this->mediator->ignitionTurnedOn();
    }

    public function stop() {
        $this->on = false;
        $this->mediator->ignitionTurnedOff();
    }

    public function isOn() {
        return $this->on;
    }

}
```

Note how the constructor establishes the two-way communication, and then how functions that perform events notify the mediator of those events.

The `Gearbox` class applies the same principles:

gearbox.php

```php
class Gearbox {

    const NEUTRAL  = 'Neutral';
    const FIRST    = '1';
    const SECOND   = '2';
    const THIRD    = '3';
    const FOURTH   = '4';
    const FIFTH    = '5';
```

```
        const REVERSE   = 'R';

        private $mediator;
        private $enabled;
        private $currentGear;

        public function __construct(EngineManagementSystem $mediator) {
            $this->this->mediator = $mediator;
            $this->enabled = false;
            $this->currentGear = Gearbox::NEUTRAL;
            $this->mediator->registerGearbox($this);
        }

        public function enable() {
            $this->enabled = true;
            $this->mediator->gearboxEnabled();
        }

        public function disable() {
            $this->enabled = false;
            $this->mediator->gearboxDisabled();
        }

        public function isEnabled() {
            return $this->enabled;
        }

        public function setGear($gear) {
            if (($this->isEnabled()) and ($this->getGear() != $gear)) {
                $this->currentGear = $gear;
                $this->mediator->gearChanged();
            }
        }
        public function getGear() {
            return $this->currentGear;
        }

    }
```

The `Accelerator` and `Brake` classes follow a similar process:

accelerator.php

```
    class Accelerator {

        private $mediator;
        private $enabled;
        private $speed;

        public function __construct(EngineManagementSystem $mediator) {
            $this-> mediator = $mediator;
            $this->enabled = false;
            $this->speed = 0;
            $this->mediator->registerAccelerator($this);
```

```php
        }

    public function enable() {
        $this->enabled = true;
        $this->mediator->acceleratorEnabled();
    }

    public function disable() {
        $this->enabled = false;
        $this->mediator->acceleratorDisabled();
    }

    public function isEnabled() {
        return $this->enabled;
    }

    public function accelerateToSpeed($speed) {
        if ($this->isEnabled()) {
            $this->speed = $speed;
            $this->mediator->acceleratorPressed();
        }
    }

    public function getSpeed() {
        return $this->speed;
    }

}
```

brake.php

```php
class Brake {

    private $mediator;
    private $enabled;
    private $applied;

    public function __construct(EngineManagementSystem $mediator) {
        $this->mediator = $mediator;
        $this->enabled = false;
        $this->applied = false;
        $this->mediator->registerBrake($this);
    }

    public function enable() {
        $this->enabled = true;
        $this->mediator->brakeEnabled();
    }

    public function disable() {
        $this->enabled = false;
        $this->mediator->brakeDisabled();
    }
```

```
    public function isEnabled() {
        return $this->enabled;
    }

    public function apply() {
        if ($this->isEnabled()) {
            $this->applied = true;
            $this->mediator->brakePressed();
        }
    }

    public function release() {
        if ($this->isEnabled()) {
            $this->applied = false;
            $this->mediator->brakeReleased();
        }
    }

}
```

So we now need the `EngineManagementSystem` class to serve as the mediator. This will hold a reference to each of the component classes with functions enabling their registration with the mediator. It also has functions to handle the interaction between the various components when particular events occur:

engine_management_system.php

```
class EngineManagementSystem {

    private $ignition;
    private $gearbox;
    private $accelerator;
    private $brake;

    private $currentSpeed;

    public function __construct() {
        $this->currentSpeed = 0;
    }


    // Functions that enable registration with this mediator...

    public function registerIgnition(Ignition $ignition) {
        $this->ignition = $ignition;
    }

    public function registerGearbox(Gearbox $gearbox) {
        $this->gearbox = $gearbox;
    }
```

```php
public function registerAccelerator(Accelerator $accelerator) {
    $this->accelerator = $accelerator;
}

public function registerBrake(Brake $brake) {
    $this->brake = $brake;
}

// Functions that handle object interactions...

public function ignitionTurnedOn() {
    $this->gearbox->enable();
    $this->accelerator->enable();
    $this->brake->enable();
}

public function ignitionTurnedOff() {
    $this->gearbox->disable();
    $this->accelerator->disable();
    $this->brake->disable();
}

public function gearboxEnabled() {
    // code…
}

public function gearboxDisabled() {
    // code…
}

public function gearChanged() {
    // code…
}

public function acceleratorEnabled() {
    // code…
}

public function acceleratorDisabled() {
    // code…
}

public function acceleratorPressed() {
    $this->brake->disable();
    while ($this->currentSpeed < $this->accelerator->getSpeed()):

        $this->currentSpeed++;

        // Set gear according to speed...
        if ($this->currentSpeed <= 10):
            $this->gearbox=>setGear(Gearbox::FIRST);

        elseif (currentSpeed <= 20):
            $this->gearbox->setGear(Gearbox::SECOND);

        elseif (currentSpeed <= 30):
```

```
                    $this->gearbox->setGear(Gearbox::THIRD);

            elseif (currentSpeed <= 50):
                $this->gearbox->setGear(Gearbox::FOURTH);

            else:
                $this->gearbox->setGear(Gearbox::FIFTH);
            endif;
        endwhile;
        $this->brake->enable();
    }

    public function brakeEnabled() {
        // code…
    }

    public function brakeDisabled() {
        // code…
    }

    public function brakePressed() {
        $this->accelerator->disable();
        $this->currentSpeed = 0;
    }

    public function brakeReleased() {
        $this->gearbox->setGear(Gearbox::FIRST);
        $this->accelerator.enable();
    }

}
```

Common uses

A common use of the *Mediator* pattern is to manage the interaction of graphical components on a dialog. This frequently involves controlling when buttons, text fields, etc. should be enabled or disabled, or for passing data between components.

Note that it may be possible to reduce the coupling further by using the *Observer* pattern in place of *Mediator*. This would mean that the component classes (i.e. Ignition, etc.) would not need to hold a reference to a mediator but would instead fire events. The EngineManagementSystem class would then be an observer of the component classes and would still be able to invoke messages on them.

19. Memento

Type	Behavioural
Purpose	Without violating encapsulation, capture and externalise an object's internal state so that it can be restored to this state later.

The Foobar Motor Company's vehicles naturally have a speedometer mounted on the dashboard, which not only records the current speed but also the previous speed. There is now a requirement for the state to be stored externally at periodic intervals (so that it could, for example, be integrated into a tachograph for goods vehicles).

However, one of the instance variables in the `Speedometer` class does not have a getter function, but to adhere to encapsulation and data-hiding principles it is correctly declared to be `private`. We also want to adhere to the principle that a class should not have multiple responsibilities, so don't want to also have to build in a state save & restore mechanism into the class. So how can we capture the state of the object?

We shall make use of a separate class that performs the state saving and restoration, which we will call `SpeedometerMemento`. This class takes a reference to the `Speedometer` object that needs to be externalised:

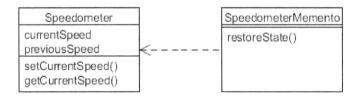

Figure 19.1 : Memento pattern

speedometer.php

```
class Speedometer {

    private $currentSpeed;
    private $previousSpeed;

    public function __construct() {
        $this->currentSpeed = 0;
        $this->previousSpeed = 0;
    }

    public function setCurrentSpeed($speed) {
        $this->previousSpeed = $this->currentSpeed;
        $this->currentSpeed = $speed;
    }

    public function getCurrentSpeed() {
        return $this->currentSpeed;
    }

    // Only defined to help testing...
    public function getPreviousSpeed() {
        return $this->previousSpeed;
    }

}
```

The `SpeedometerMemento` class now uses object serialization for the state saving and restoration:

speedometer_memento.php

```
class SpeedometerMemento {

    const SPEEDO_FILE = 'speedofile.data';

    public function __construct(Speedometer $speedometer) {
        // Serialize...
        file_put_contents(SpeedometerMemento::SPEEDO_FILE,
                          serialize($speedometer));
    }

    public function restoreState() {
        // Unserialize...
        return unserialize(
                    file_get_contents(
                        SpeedometerMemento::SPEEDO_FILE));
    }

}
```

We can check this works by setting a speed, storing it as a memento, changing the speed and then restoring back from the memento:

```
$speedo = new Speedometer();

$speedo->setCurrentSpeed(50);
$speedo->setCurrentSpeed(100);

// Save the state of 'speedo'...
$memento = new SpeedometerMemento($speedo);

// Change the state of 'speedo'...
$speedo->setCurrentSpeed(80);

// Restore the state of 'speedo'...
$speedo = $memento->restoreState();
```

Running the above should result in showing a current speed of 100 and a previous speed of 50. The main disadvantage of this approach is that writing to and reading from a disk file will have a performance impact.

20. Observer

Type	Behavioural
Purpose	Define a one-to-many dependency between objects so that when one object changes its state, all its dependants are notified and updated automatically.

The Foobar Motor Company has decided that an alert should sound to the driver whenever a certain speed is exceeded. They also envisage that other things may need to happen depending upon the current speed (such as an automatic gearbox selecting the appropriate gear to match the speed). But they realise the need to keep objects loosely-coupled, so naturally don't wish the `Speedometer` class to have any direct knowledge of speed monitors or automatic gearboxes (or any other future class that might be interested in the speed a vehicle is travelling).

The *Observer* pattern enables a loose-coupling to be established between a 'subject' (the object that is of interest; `Speedometer` on our example) and its 'observers' (any other class that needs to be kept informed when interesting stuff happens).

One means of achieving this is by creating an abstract `Observable` class and an `Observer` interface:

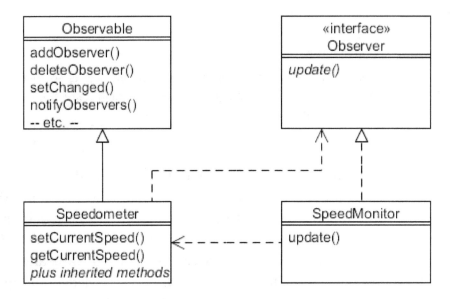

Figure 20.1 : Observer pattern

The 'subject' (Speedometer) can have multiple observers (which can in fact be any class that implements the Observer interface, not just SpeedMonitor objects).

The Observer interface only needs one function, which will get called whenever it gets notified that something has been updated:

observer.php

```
interface Observer {
    public function update(Observable $observable);
}
```

The Observable abstract class defines functions to register and notify observers.

Observable.php

```php
abstract class Observable {

    private $observers = array();
    private $changed;

    public function __construct() {
        $this->changed = false;
    }

    public function addObserver(Observer $observer) {
        array_push($this->observers, $observer);
    }

    public function deleteObserver(Observer $observer) {
        unset($this->observers[$observer]);
    }

    public function deleteObservers() {
        $this->observers = array();
    }

    public function notifyObservers() {
        if ($this->hasChanged()):
            foreach ($this->observers as $observer):
                $observer->update($this);
            endforeach;
        endif;
        $this->clearChanged();
    }

    public function hasChanged() {
        return $this->changed;
    }

    protected function setChanged() {
        $this->changed = true;
    }

    protected function clearChanged() {
        $this->changed = false;
    }

}
```

The Speedometer class looks like this[1]:

speedometer.php

```php
class Speedometer extends Observable {
```

---

[1]Unlike the version in the *Memento* pattern chapter, there is no variable to record the previous speed as it is irrelevant to this example.

```
        private $currentSpeed;

        public function __construct() {
            $this->currentSpeed = 0;
        }

        public function setCurrentSpeed($speed) {
            $this->currentSpeed = $speed;

            // Tell all observers so they know speed has changed...
            $this->setChanged();
            $this->notifyObservers();
        }

        public function getCurrentSpeed() {
            return $this->currentSpeed;
        }


    }
```

The `Speedometer` class extends our `Observable` class and thus inherits for our convenience its functions concerned with the registration and notification of observers. For our example, whenever the speed has changed we invoke the inherited `setChanged()` and `notifyObservers()` functions which takes care of the notifications for us.

The `SpeedMonitor` class implements the `Observer` interface and has the appropriate code for its required function `update()`:

speed_monitor.php

```
    class SpeedMonitor implements Observer {

        private $speed_to_alert = 70;
        private $speeding = false;

        public function update(Observable $speedo) {
            if ($speedo->getCurrentSpeed() > $this->speed_to_alert()):
                $this->speeding = true;
            else:
                $this->speeding = false;
            endif;
        }

        public function isSpeeding() {
            return $this->speeding;
```

```
        }
    }
```

Client programs simply pass a `SpeedMonitor` reference to an instance of `Speedometer`:

```
Create a monitor...
$monitor = new SpeedMonitor();

// Create a speedometer and register the monitor to it...
$speedo = new Speedometer();
$speedo->addObserver($monitor);

// Drive at different speeds...
$speedo->setCurrentSpeed(50);
$speedo->setCurrentSpeed(70);
$speedo->setCurrentSpeed(40);
$speedo->setCurrentSpeed(100);
$speedo->setCurrentSpeed(69);
```

The real power behind the *Observer* pattern is that any type of class can now become a monitor provided they implement the `Observer` interface, and without requiring any changes to be made to `Speedometer`. Let's create a simulation of an automatic gearbox:

```
class AutomaticGearbox implements Observer {

    private $gear;

    public function update(Observable $speedo) {
        if ($speedo->getCurrentSpeed() <= 10):
            $this->gear = 1;

        elseif ($speedo->getCurrentSpeed() <= 20):
            $this->gear = 2;

        elseif ($speedo->getCurrentSpeed() <= 30):
            $this->gear = 3;

        else:
            $this->gear = 4;
        endif;
    }

    public function getGear() {
        return $this->gear;
    }
}
```

Our client program can now just add this as an additional observer and get notifications of speed changes as well:

```
$auto = new AutomaticGearbox();
$speedo->addObserver($auto);
```

21. State

Type	Behavioural
Purpose	Allow an object to alter its behaviour when its internal state changes. The object will appear to change its class.

The Foobar Motor Company's vehicles each have a digital clock fitted that displays the current date and time. These values will need to be reset from time to time (such as after a change of battery) and this is accomplished by means of a particular knob on the dashboard. When the knob is initially pressed, the 'year' value can be set. Turning the knob to the left (i.e. anti-clockwise) causes the previous year to be show, whereas turning it to the right goes forward one year. When the knob is pressed again the year value becomes 'set' and the set-up process then automatically allows the month value to be set, also by making appropriate left or right movements with the knob.

This process continues for the day of the month, the hour and the minute. The following table summarises the flow of events:

User Action	What Happens
Push knob	Clock goes into 'setup' mode for setting **year**
Rotate knob left	1 is deducted from the **year** value
Rotate knob right	1 is added to the **year** value
Push knob	Year now set and automatically transitions into **month** set-up
Rotate knob left	1 is deducted from the **month** value
Rotate knob right	1 is added to the **month** value
Push knob	Month now set and automatically transitions into **day** set-up
Rotate knob left	1 is deducted from the **day** value
Rotate knob right	1 is added to the **day** value

Push knob	Day now set and automatically transitions into **hour** set-up
Rotate knob left	1 is deducted from the **hour** value
Rotate knob right	1 is added to the **hour** value
Push knob	Hour now set and automatically transitions into **minute** set-up
Rotate knob left	1 is deducted from the **minute** value
Rotate knob right	1 is added to the **minute** value
Push knob	Minute now set and automatically transitions for into '**finished**' mode
Push knob	Displays set date & time

From the above steps it is clear that different parts of the date & time get set when the knob is turned or pressed, and that there are transitions between those parts. A naive approach when coding a class to accomplish this would be to have a 'mode' variable and then a series of if...else... statements in each function, which might look like this:

```
// *** DON'T DO THIS! ***
public function rotateKnobLeft() {
    if ($mode == YEAR_MODE):
        $year--;
    elseif ($mode == MONTH_MODE):
        $month--;
    elseif ($mode == DAY_MODE):
        $day--;
    elseif ($mode == HOUR_MODE):
        $hour--;
    elseif ($mode == MINUTE_MODE):
        $minute--;
    endif;
}
```

The problem with code such as the above is that the if...else... conditions would have to be repeated in each action function (i.e. rotateKnobRight(), pushKnob(), etc.). Apart from making the code look unwieldy it also becomes hard to maintain, as if for example we now need to record seconds we would need to change multiple parts of the class.

The *State* pattern enables a hierarchy to be established that allows for state transitions such as necessitated by our clock setting example. We will create a ClockSetup class that initiates the states through the interface ClockSetupState, which has an implementing class for each individual state:

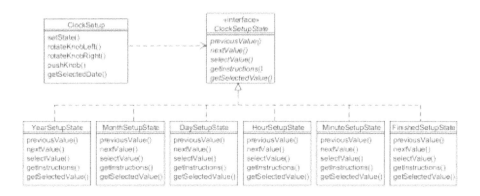

Figure 21.1 : State pattern

The ClockSetupState interface defines functions for handling changes to the state, plus functions that can provide user instructions and return the actual selected value:

clock_setup_state.php

```
interface ClockSetupState {
    public function previousValue();
    public function nextValue();
    public function selectValue();

    public function getInstructions();
    public function getSelectedValue();
}
```

Looking first at YearSetupState, you will notice that it takes a reference to a ClockSetup object (to be defined later) in the constructor (which is known in the language of design patterns as its 'context') and manages the setting of the year. Note in particular in the `selectValue()` function how it transitions internally to a different state:

year_setup_state.php

```php
class YearSetupState implements ClockSetupState {

    private $clockSetup;
    private $year;

    public function __construct(ClockSetup $clockSetup) {
        $this->clockSetup = $clockSetup;
        $this->year = date('Y'); // default to current year
    }

    public function previousValue() {
        $this->year--;
    }

    public function nextValue() {
        $this->year++;
    }

    public function selectValue() {
        $this->clockSetup.setState
          ($this->clockSetup->getMonthSetupState());
    }

    public function getInstructions() {
        return 'Please set the year...';
    }

    public function getSelectedValue() {
        return $this->year;
    }

}
```

The other date & time state classes follow a similar process, each transitioning to the next appropriate state when required:

month_setup_state.php

```php
class MonthSetupState implements ClockSetupState {

    private $clockSetup;
    private $month;

    public function __construct(ClockSetup $clockSetup) {
        $this->clockSetup = $clockSetup;
        $this->month = date('n'); // default to current month
```

```
        }

        public function previousValue() {
            $this->month--;
        }

        public function nextValue() {
            $this->month++;
        }

        public function selectValue() {
            $this->clockSetup.setState
               ($this->clockSetup->getDaySetupState());
        }

        public function getInstructions() {
            return 'Please set the month...';
        }

        public function getSelectedValue() {
            return $this->month;
        }

    }
```

day_setup_state.php

```
    class DaySetupState implements ClockSetupState {

        private $clockSetup;
        private $day;

        public function __construct(ClockSetup $clockSetup) {
            $this->clockSetup = $clockSetup;
            $this->day = date('j'); // default to current day
        }

        public function previousValue() {
            $this->day--;
        }

        public function nextValue() {
            $this->day++;
        }

        public function selectValue() {
            $this->clockSetup.setState
               ($this->clockSetup->getHourSetupState());
        }

        public function getInstructions() {
            return 'Please set the day...';
        }
```

```php
    public function getSelectedValue() {
        return $this->day;
    }

}
```

hour_setup_state.php

```php
class HourSetupState implements ClockSetupState {

    private $clockSetup;
    private $hour;

    public function __construct(ClockSetup $clockSetup) {
        $this->clockSetup = $clockSetup;
        $this->hour = date('G'); // default to current hour
    }

    public function previousValue() {
        $this->hour--;
    }

    public function nextValue() {
        $this->hour++;
    }

    public function selectValue() {
        $this->clockSetup.setState
           ($this->clockSetup->getMinuteSetupState());
    }

    public function getInstructions() {
        return 'Please set the hour...';
    }

    public function getSelectedValue() {
        return $this->hour;
    }

}
```

minute_setup_state.php

```php
class MinuteSetupState implements ClockSetupState {

    private $clockSetup;
    private $minute;

    public function __construct(ClockSetup $clockSetup) {
        $this->clockSetup = $clockSetup;
        $this->minute = date('i'); // default to current minute
    }
```

```
    public function previousValue() {
        $this->minute--;
    }

    public function nextValue() {
        $this->minute++;
    }

    public function selectValue() {
        $this->clockSetup.setState
            ($this->clockSetup->getFinishedSetupState());
    }

    public function getInstructions() {
        return 'Please set the minute...';
    }

    public function getSelectedValue() {
        return $this->minute;
    }

}
```

This just leaves the `FinishedSetupState` class which doesn't need to transition to a different state:

finished_setup_state.php

```
class FinishedSetupState implements ClockSetupState {

    private $clockSetup;

    public function __construct(ClockSetup $clockSetup) {
        $this->clockSetup = $clockSetup;
    }

    public function previousValue() {
        // No op
    }

    public function nextValue() {
        // No op
    }

    public function selectValue() {
        // No op
    }

    public function getInstructions() {
        return 'Press knob to view selected date...';
    }
```

```
        public function getSelectedValue() {
            // No op
        }

    }
```

As mentioned, the 'context' class is `ClockSetup`, which holds references to each state and forwards to whichever is the current state:

clock_setup.php

```
    class ClockSetup {

        // The various states the setup can be in...
        private $yearState;
        private $monthState;
        private $dayState;
        private $hourState;
        private $minuteState;
        private $finishedState;

        // The current state we are in...
        private $currentState;

        public function __construct() {
            $this->yearState = new YearSetupState($this);
            $this->monthState = new MonthSetupState($this);
            $this->dayState = new DaySetupState($this);
            $this->hourState = new HourSetupState($this);
            $this->minuteState = new MinuteSetupState($this);
            $this->finishedState = new FinishedSetupState($this);

            // Initial state is to set the year
            $this->setState($this->yearState);
        }

        public function setState(ClockSetupState $state) {
            $this->currentState = $state;
        }

        public function rotateKnobLeft() {
            $this->currentState->previousValue();
        }

        public function rotateKnobRight() {
            $this->currentState->nextValue();
        }

        public function pushKnob() {
            $this->currentState->selectValue();
        }
```

```php
    public function getYearSetupState() {
        return $this->yearState;
    }

    public function getMonthSetupState() {
        return $this->monthState;
    }

    public function getDaySetupState() {
        return $this->dayState;
    }

    public function getHourSetupState() {
        return $this->hourState;
    }

    public  function getMinuteSetupState() {
        return $this->minuteState;
    }

    public function getFinishedSetupState() {
        return $this->finishedState;
    }

    public function getSelectedDate() {
        $date = mktime($this->hourState->getSelectedValue(),
                       $this->minuteState->getSelectedValue(),
                       0,
                       $this->monthState->getSelectedValue(),
                       $this->dayState->getSelectedValue(),
                       $this->yearState->getSelectedValue()
                       );
         return date('r', $date);
    }

}
```

We can simulate a user's example actions like this:

```php
$clockSetup = new ClockSetup();

// Setup starts in 'year' state
$clockSetup->rotateKnobRight();
$clockSetup->pushKnob(); // 1 year on

// Setup should now be in 'month' state
$clockSetup->rotateKnobRight();
$clockSetup->rotateKnobRight();
$clockSetup->pushKnob(); // 2 months on

// Setup should now be in 'day' state
$clockSetup->rotateKnobRight();
$clockSetup->rotateKnobRight();
$clockSetup->rotateKnobRight();
```

```php
$clockSetup->pushKnob(); // 3 days on

// Setup should now be in 'hour' state
$clockSetup->rotateKnobLeft();
$clockSetup->rotateKnobLeft();
$clockSetup->pushKnob(); // 2 hours back

// Setup should now be in 'minute' state
$clockSetup->rotateKnobRight();
$clockSetup->pushKnob(); // 1 minute on

// Setup should now be in 'finished' state
$clockSetup->pushKnob();

// In HTML display the selected date
<?php echo $clockSetup->getSelectedDate(); ?>
```

22. Strategy

Type	Behavioural
Purpose	Define a family of algorithms, encapsulate each one, and make them interchangeable. *Strategy* lets the algorithm vary independently from clients that use it.

The Foobar Motor Company wishes to implement a new type of automatic gearbox for their cars that will be able to be switched between its standard mode and a special 'sport' mode. The different modes will base the decision of which gear should be selected depending upon the speed of travel, size of the engine and whether it is turbocharged. And it's quite possible they will want other modes in the future, such as for off-road driving.

Just as with the discussion in the chapter for the *State* pattern, it would be inflexible to use a series of if...else... statements to control the different gearbox modes directly inside our vehicle classes. Instead, we shall encapsulate the concept that varies and define a separate hierarchy so that each different gearbox mode is a separate class, each in effect being a different 'strategy' that gets applied. This approach allows the actual strategy being used to be isolated from the vehicle. In our example, we shall only apply this to the cars:

Figure 22.1 : Strategy pattern

The `GearboxStrategy` interface defines the function to control the gear:

gearbox_strategy.php

```
interface GearboxStrategy {
    public function ensureCorrectGear(Engine $engine, $speed);
}
```

There are two implementing classes; `StandardGearboxStrategy` and `SportGearboxStrategy`:

standard_gearbox_strategy.php

```
class StandardGearboxStrategy implements GearboxStrategy {

    public function ensureCorrectGear(Engine $engine, $speed) {
        $engineSize = $engine->getSize();
        $turbo = $engine->isTurbo();

        //  Some complicated code to determine correct gear
        //  setting based on $engineSize, $turbo & $speed, etc.
        //  ... omitted ...

        return 'Working out correct gear at ' . $speed .
                        'mph for a STANDARD gearbox');
    }

}
```

sport_gearbox_strategy.php

```
class SportGearboxStrategy implements GearboxStrategy {

    public function ensureCorrectGear(Engine $engine, $speed) {
        $engineSize = $engine->getSize();
        $turbo = $engine->isTurbo();

        //  Some complicated code to determine correct gear
        //  setting based on $engineSize, $turbo & $speed, etc.
        //  ... omitted ...

        return 'Working out correct gear at ' . $speed .
                        'mph for a SPORT gearbox');
    }

}
```

Our `AbstractCar` class is defined to hold a reference to the interface type (i.e. `GearboxStrategy`) and provide accessor functions so different strategies can be switched. There is also a `setSpeed()` function that delegates to whatever strategy is in effect. The pertinent code is marked in bold:

```
abstract class AbstractCar extends AbstractVehicle {

    private $gearboxStrategy;

    public function __construct(Engine $engine,
                                $colour = Vehicle::UNPAINTED) {
        parent::__construct($engine, $colour);

        //  Starts in standard gearbox mode (more economical)
        $this->gearboxStrategy = new StandardGearboxStrategy();
    }

    // Allow the gearbox strategy to be changed...
    public function setGearboxStrategy(GearboxStrategy $gs) {
        $this->gearboxStrategy = $gs;
    }

    public function getGearboxStrategy() {
        return $this->getGearboxStrategy;
    }

    public function setSpeed($speed) {
        // Delegate to strategy in effect...
        $this->gearboxStrategy->ensureCorrectGear(
                        $this->getEngine(),$this->speed);
    }

}
```

Client programs just set the required strategy:

```
$myCar = new Sport(new StandardEngine(2000));
$myCar->setSpeed(20);
$myCar->setSpeed(40);

// Switching on sports mode gearbox...
$myCar->setGearboxStrategy(new SportGearboxStrategy());
$myCar->setSpeed(20);
$myCar->setSpeed(40);
```

23. Template Method

Type	Behavioural
Purpose	Define the skeleton of an algorithm in a function, deferring some steps to subclasses. *Template Method* lets subclasses redefine certain steps of an algorithm without changing the algorithm's structure.

Each vehicle made by the Foobar Motor Company needs a small number of printed booklets to be produced and provided to the buyer, such as an Owner's Manual and a Service History booklet. The way booklets are produced always follows the same set of steps, but each different type of booklet might need to do each of the individual steps in a slightly different way.

The *Template Method* pattern enables the definition of one or more abstract functions that are called through a 'template method' (function). The simple hierarchy is as follows:

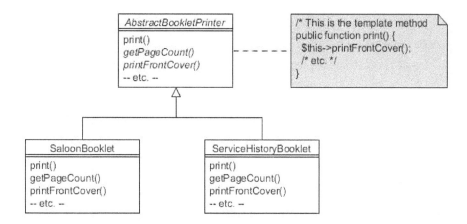

Figure 23.1 : Template Method pattern

The `AbstractBookletPrinter` class defines several `protected abstract` functions and one `public final` 'template method' that makes use of the abstract functions (the function is made `final` to prevent it from being overridden):

abstract_booklet_printer.php

```
abstract class AbstractBookletPrinter {

    protected abstract function getPageCount();
    protected abstract function printFrontCover();
    protected abstract function printTableOfContents();
    protected abstract function printPage($pageNumber);
    protected abstract function printIndex();
    protected abstract function printBackCover();

    // This is the 'template method'
    public final void printBooklet() {
        $this->printFrontCover();
        $this->printTableOfContents();
        for ($i = 1; $i <= $this->getPageCount(); $i++):
            $this->printPage($i);
        endfor;
        $this->printIndex();
        $this->printBackCover();
    }

}
```

Each concrete subclass now only needs to provide the implementing code for each abstract function, for example the `SaloonBooklet` class below:

saloon_booklet.php

```
class SaloonBooklet extends AbstractBookletPrinter {

    protected function getPageCount() {
        return 100;
    }

    protected function printFrontCover() {
        return 'Printing front cover for Saloon car booklet';
    }

    protected function printTableOfContents() {
        return 'Printing table of contents for Saloon car booklet';
    }

    protected function printPage($pageNumber) {
        return 'Printing page ' + $pageNumber +
```

```
            ' for Saloon car booklet');
    }

    protected function printIndex() {
        return 'Printing index for Saloon car booklet';
    }

    protected function printBackCover() {
        return 'Printing back cover for Saloon car booklet';
    }

}
```

The `ServiceHistoryBooklet` **is very similar:**

service_history_booklet.php

```
class ServiceHistoryBooklet extends AbstractBookletPrinter {

    protected function getPageCount() {
        return 12;
    }

    protected function printFrontCover() {
        return 'Printing front cover for service history booklet';
    }

    protected function printTableOfContents() {
        return 'Printing table of contents for service history
                                          booklet';
    }

    protected function printPage($pageNumber) {
        return 'Printing page ' + $pageNumber +
            ' for service history booklet');
    }

    protected function printIndex() {
        return 'Printing index for service history booklet';
    }

    protected function printBackCover() {
        return 'Printing back cover for service history booklet';
    }

}
```

While it is not essential from the point of view of the pattern for the abstract functions to be `protected`, it is often the case that this is the most appropriate access level to assign since they are only intended for over-riding and not for direct invocation by client objects.

Also note that it's perfectly acceptable for some of the functions called from the 'template method' to not be abstract but have a default implementation provided. But when at least one abstract function is being called, it qualifies as the *Template Method* pattern.

Client programs merely need to instantiate the required concrete class and invoke the `printBooklet()` function:

```
$saloonBooklet = new SaloonBooklet();
$saloonBooklet->printBooklet();

$serviceBooklet = new ServiceHistoryBooklet();
$serviceBooklet->printBooklet();
```

24. Visitor

Type	Behavioural
Purpose	Represent a function to be performed on the elements of an object structure. *Visitor* lets you define a new function without changing the classes of the elements on which it operates.

Sometimes a class hierarchy and its code become substantive, and yet it is known that future requirements will be inevitable. An example for the Foobar Motor Company is the `Engine` hierarchy which looks like this:

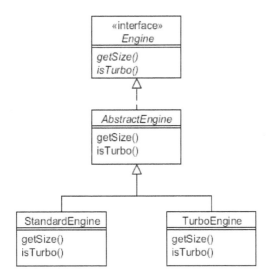

Figure 24.1 : Engine class hierarchy

In reality, the code within the `AbstractEngine` class is likely to be composed of a multitude of individual components, such as a camshaft, piston, some spark plugs, etc. If we need to add some functionality that traverses these components then the natural way is to just add a function to `AbstractEngine`. But maybe we know there are potentially many such new requirements and we would rather not have to keep adding functions directly into the hierarchy?

The *Visitor* pattern enables us to define just one additional function to add into the class hierarchy in such a way that lots of different types of new functionality can be added without any further changes. This is accomplished by means of a technique known as "double-despatch", whereby the invoked function issues a call-back to the invoking object.

The technique requires first the definition of an interface we shall call `EngineVisitor`:

engine_visitor.php

```
interface EngineVisitor {
    public function visitCamshaft(Camshaft $camshaft);
    public function visitEngine(Engine $engine);
    public function visitPiston(Piston $piston);
    public function visitSparkPlug(SparkPlug $sparkPlug);
}
```

We will also define an interface called `Visitable` with an `acceptEngineVisitor()` function:

visitable.php

```
public interface Visitable {
    public function acceptEngineVisitor(EngineVisitor $visitor);
}
```

The `Engine` interface you have met in previous chapters (although we will modify it slightly for this chapter). The `Camshaft`, `Piston` and `SparkPlug` classes are each very simple, as follows:

camshaft.php

```
class Camshaft implements Visitable {
    public function acceptEngineVisitor(EngineVisitor $visitor) {
        $visitor->visitCamshaft($this);
    }
}
```

piston.php

```
class Piston implements Visitable {
    public function acceptEngineVisitor(EngineVisitor $visitor) {
        $visitor->visitPiston($this);
    }
}
```

sparkplug.php

```
class SparkPlug implements Visitable {
    public function acceptEngineVisitor(EngineVisitor $visitor) {
        $visitor->visitSparkPlug($this);
    }
}
```

As you can see, each of these classes defines a function called `acceptEngineVisitor()` that takes a reference to an `EngineVisitor` object as its argument. All the function does is invoke the `visit()` function of the passed-in `EngineVisitor`, passing back the object instance.

Our modified `Engine` interface also now implements `visitable`:

engine.php

```
public interface Engine extends Visitable {
    public function getSize();
    public function isTurbo();
}
```

The `AbstractEngine` class therefore needs to implement this new function, which in this case traverses the individual components (camshaft, piston, spark plugs) invoking `acceptEngineVisitor()` on each:

abstract_engine.php

```
abstract class AbstractEngine implements Engine {

    private $size;
    private $turbo;
```

```
    private $camshaft;
    private $piston;
    private $sparkPlugs = array();

    public function __construct($size, $turbo) {
        $this->size = $size;
        $this->turbo = $turbo;

        // Create a camshaft, piston and 4 spark plugs...`
        $this->camshaft = new Camshaft();
        $this->piston = new Piston()
        $this->sparkPlugs[0] = new SparkPlug();
        $this->sparkPlugs[1] = new SparkPlug();
        $this->sparkPlugs[2] = new SparkPlug();
        $this->sparkPlugs[3] = new SparkPlug();
    }

    public function getSize() {
        return $this->size;
    }

    public function isTurbo() {
        return $this->turbo;
    }

    public function acceptEngineVisitor(EngineVisitor $visitor) {
        // Visit each component first...
        $this->camshaft->acceptEngineVisitor($visitor);
        $this->piston->acceptEngineVisitor($visitor);
        foreach ($this->sparkPlugs as $sparkPlug):
            $sparkPlug->acceptEngineVisitor($visitor);
        endforeach;

        // Now visit the receiver...
        return $visitor->visitEngine($this);
    }

    public function toString() {
        return get_class($this) . ' (' + (string)$this->size . ')');
    }

}
```

Now we shall create an actual implementation of EngineVisitor so you can see how we can easily add additional functionality to engines without any further changes to any engine hierarchy class. The first thing we shall do is to define some clever electronic gizmo that can be attached to an engine that will automatically check each component and diagnose any faults. We therefore define the EngineDiagnostics class:

engine_diagnostics.php

```php
class EngineDiagnostics implements EngineVisitor {

    public void visitCamshaft(Camshaft camshaft) {
        return 'Diagnosing the camshaft';
    }

    public void visitEngine(Engine engine) {
        retur 'Diagnosing the unit engine';
    }

    public void visitPiston(Piston piston) {
        return 'Diagnosing the piston';
    }

    public void visitSparkPlug(SparkPlug sparkPlug) {
        return 'Diagnosing a single spark plug';
    }

}
```

We also want to print an inventory of how many of each type of component there is within an engine, so we also have an EngineInventory class:

engine_inventory.php

```php
class EngineInventory implements EngineVisitor {

    private $camshaftCount;
    private $pistonCount;
    private $sparkPlugCount;

    public function __construct() {
        $this->camshaftCount = 0;
        $this->pistonCount = 0;
        $this->sparkPlugCount = 0;
    }

    public function visitCampshaft(Camshaft $camshaft) {
        $this->camshaftCount++;
    }

    public function visitEngine(Engine $engine) {
        return 'The engine has: ' .
                $this->camshaftCount . ' camshaft(s), ' .
                $this->pistonCount . ' piston(s), and ' .
                $this->sparkPlugCount . ' spark plug(s)';
    }

    public function visit(Piston $piston) {
        $this->pistonCount++;
```

```
    }

    public function visit(SparkPlug sparkPlug) {
        $this->sparkPlugCount++;
    }

}
```

The following diagram summarises how all of these classes interact:

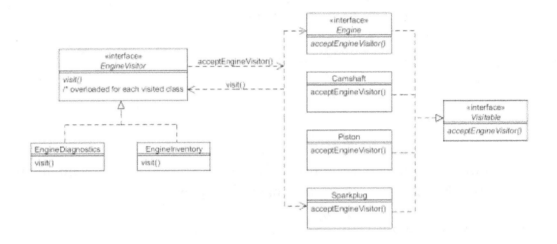

Figure 24.2 : Visitor pattern

Client programs now only need to invoke the `acceptEngineVisitor()` function on an instance of `Engine`, passing in the appropriate `EngineVisitor` object:

```
// Create an engine...
$engine = new StandardEngine(1300);

// Run diagnostics on the engine...
$engine->acceptEngineVisitor(new EngineDiagnostics());
```

The output should show:

```
Diagnosing the unit engine
```

And to obtain the inventory (using the same `Engine` instance):

```
// Run inventory on the engine...
$engine->acceptEngineVisitor(new EngineInventory());
```

The output should show:

```
The engine has: 1 camshaft(s), 1 piston(s), and 4 spark plug(s)
```

Part V. Other Useful Patterns

This part describes three additional patterns you should find useful in practical applications.

- *Null Object*: Define a class that enables the processing of `null` values;

- *Simple Factory*: Delegate the instantiation of objects;

- *Model View Controller*: Separate a user interface component's screen representation from its underlying data and functionality;

25. Null Object

When iterating through a collection of objects such as an array, you sometimes have to deal with the situation of some of those objects being `null`, where of course you cannot then invoke a function on it. Sometimes, the only way around this is to specifically test for `null` before performing an operation, which puts an extra onus on the programmer.

Suppose a vehicle's instrument panel contains three slots for warning lights (such as for low oil level or low brake fluid level). A particular vehicle might only use these two lights, with the third slot empty, represented by `null` within PHP. Looping through the slots would require a specific test to prevent an error being thrown:

```
// OilLevelLight & BrakeFluidLight are each types of WarningLight
$lights = array();
$lights[0] = new OilLevelLight();
$lights[1] = new BrakeFluidLight();
$lights[2] = null; // empty slot

foreach ($lights as $light):
    if ($light != null):
        $light->turnOn();
        $light->turnOff();
    endif;
endforeach;
```

An approach that can help prevent the need to test for `null` is to create a 'null object' class as part of the class hierarchy. This class will implement the same interface but perform no actual function, as illustrated in the following figure:

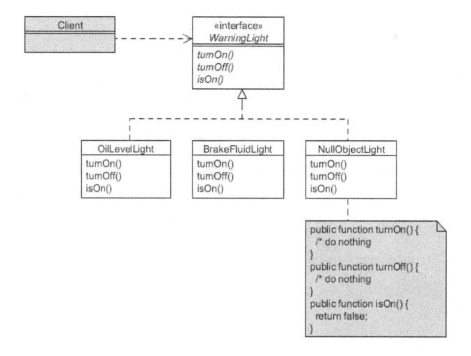

Figure 25.1 : Null Object pattern

The `WarningLight` interface defines the functions `turnOn()`, `turnOff()` and `isOn()`:

warning_light.php

```
interface WarningLight {
    public function turnOn();
    public function turnOff();
    public function isOn();
}
```

The `OilLightLevel` and `BrakeFluidLevel` classes each implement the `WarningLight` interface and provide the appropriate code to switch the light on or off:

oil_level_light.php

```php
class OilLevelLight implements WarningLight {

    private $on;

    public function turnOn() {
        $this->on = true;
    }

    public function turnOff() {
        $this->on = false;
    }

    public function isOn() {
        return $this->on;
    }
}
```

brake_fluid_level.php

```php
class BrakeFluidLight implements WarningLight {

    private $on;

    public function turnOn() {
        $this->on = true;
    }

    public function turnOff() {
        $this->on = false;
    }

    public function isOn() {
        return $this->on;
    }
}
```

For the *Null Object* pattern we also create a `NullObjectLight` class that implements the `WarningLight` interface but performs no actual processing:

null_object_light.php

```php
class NullObjectLight implements WarningLight {

    public function turnOn() {
        // Do nothing...
    }

    public function turnOff() {
        // Do nothing...
```

```
    }

    public function isOn() {
        return false;
    }
}
```

Now our client code can be simplified since we no longer need to test if a slot is `null`, provided we make use of the null object:

```
$lights = new WarningLight[3];
$lights[0] = new OilLevelLight();
$lights[1] = new BrakeFluidLight();
$lights[2] = new NullObjectLight(); // empty slot

// No need to test for null...
foreach ($lights as $light):
    $light->turnOn();
    $light->turnOff();
endforeach;
```

Note that for *Null Object* getter functions you will need to return whatever seems sensible as a default; hence above the `isOn()` function returns `false` since it represents a non-existent light.

26. Simple Factory

In the main section of this book we looked at both the *Factory Method* pattern and the *Abstract Factory* pattern. The *Simple Factory* pattern[1] is a commonly used simplified means of delegating the instantiation of objects to a specific class (the 'factory').

We shall assume here that the Foobar Motor Company manufactures two types of gearbox; an automatic gearbox and a manual gearbox. Client programs might need to create one or the other based upon a condition, as illustrated by the following code fragment (assuming the classes are defined within a class hierarchy):

```
if ($typeWanted == 'automatic'):
    $selectedGearbox = new AutomaticGearbox();
else:
    $selectedGearbox = new ManualGearbox();
endif;

// Do something with $selectedGearbox...
```

While the above code will of course work, what happens if more than one client program needs to perform a similar selection? We would have to repeat the if...else... statements in each client program, and if a new type of gearbox is subsequently manufactured we would have to track down every place the if...else... block is used.

Remembering the principle of encapsulating the concept that varies, we can instead delegate the selection and instantiation process to a specific class, known as the 'factory', just for that purpose. Client programs then only make use of the create() function of the factory, as illustrated in the diagram below:

---

[1]Some authors state that *Simple Factory* is more of an object-oriented programming idiom rather than a full-fledged pattern.

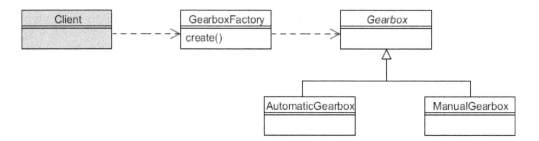

Figure 26.1 : Simple Factory pattern

The interface `Gearbox` in our example merely defines a simple getter function:

gearbox.php

```
interface Gearbox {
    public function getCurrentGear();
}
```

The `AutomaticGearbox` and `ManualGearbox` classes each implement `Gearbox` for their respective types:

automatic_gearbox.php

```
class AutomaticGearbox implements Gearbox {
    public function getCurrentGear () {
        return 'Current gear for the AUTOMATIC gearbox';
    }
}
```

manual_gearbox.php

```
class ManualGearbox implements Gearbox {
    public function getCurrentGear () {
        return 'Current gear for the MANUAL gearbox';
    }
}
```

We now need to create our `GearboxFactory` class that is capable of instantiating the appropriate `Gearbox`:

gearbox_factory.php

```
class GearboxFactory {

    const AUTOMATIC = 1;
    const MANUAL = 2;

    public static function create($type) {
        if ($type == GearboxFactory::AUTOMATIC):
            return new AutomaticGearbox();
        else:
            return new ManualGearbox();
        endif;
    }

}
```

The `create()` function takes care of the selection and instantiation, and thus isolates each client program from repeating code. We have made the function `static` purely for convenience; it is not a requirement of the pattern.

Client programs now obtain the type of gearbox by means of the factory:

```
// Create an automatic gearbox
$auto = GearboxFactory::create(GearboxFactory::AUTOMATIC);

// Create a manual gearbox
$manual = GearboxFactory::create(GearboxFactory::MANUAL);
```

27. Model View Controller

The Foobar Motor Company would like to supply a simple stock management function for their car dealers, which shows the cars currently in stock and allows more to be added.

The user interface will look like this:

Car Management

Add to stock

Type: Saloon ▾ Engine: 1300 ▾ Colour: Blue ▾ [Submit]

Cars in stock

- Coupe (StandardEngine(1600), Black)
- Saloon (StandardEngine(1300), Blue)
- Sport (StandardEngine(2000), Red)

Figure 27.1 Car Management

The Cars in stock section will initially be empty, but items will appear each time the Submit button is clicked using the selected car criteria. The data is saved to a file.

This is a straightforward program that would be entirely possible to code within a single PHP file. But as graphical applications become more complex, it greatly simplifies development and maintenance if you separate the major parts of the application.

The *Model View Controller* pattern (often abbreviated to MVC) is a way of achieving a looser coupling between the constituent parts, and is a tried-and-tested approach to graphical applications. There are typically three parts at play in GUI applications:

1. *The "Model".* This is the 'data' (i.e. state) and associated application or 'business' logic. In our example, this comprises loading and storing the stock list, adding new items to stock, and functions to return them to other objects.

2. *The "View".* This is the graphical display, as shown in the figure. It gets its data from the *Model.*

3. *The "Controller".* This is the part that responds to all user input (such as button clicks) and liaises with both the *Model* and the *View.*

Each of the above three parts will be in a separate class, which can be visualised as follows:

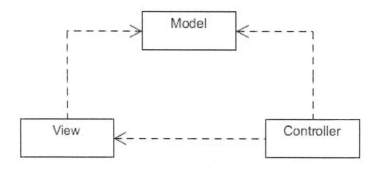

Figure 27.3 : MVC classses and thier interaction

These classes interrelate in the following way:

• `Model` contains the "meat" of the application. It manages the data and business logic, but has no knowledge of the *View* or the *Controller;*

• `View` defines the graphical front-end. It holds a reference to `Model` so it can obtain the data necessary for displaying. The actual display might be performed by a template of HTML;

- Controller holds a reference to both Model and View. It handles button clicks by telling the *Model* that a new car needs to be added and telling the *View* that it needs to refresh its display because of this.

Just as with the other patterns described in this book, there are variations in how MVC can be structured, and the above might be described as the 'classical' approach.

We shall start with the *Model*, which in our case is the class CarModel. The important point is that it has direct knowledge of neither the *View* nor the *Controller*, and could therefore be plugged into all sorts of other applications without any changes being required.

car_model.php

```
class CarModel {

    const DB_FILE      = 'cars-in-stock.dat';

    const SALOON       = 'Saloon';
    const COUPE        = 'Coupe';
    const SPORT        = 'Sport';

    const ENGINE_1300  = 1300;
    const ENGINE_1600  = 1600;
    const ENGINE_2000  = 2000;

    private $carTypesAvailable = array(
        CarModel::SALOON, CarModel::COUPE, CarModel::SPORT);
    private $engineSizesAvailable = array(
        CarModel:: ENGINE_1300, CarModel:: ENGINE_1600,
                                        CarModel:: ENGINE_2000);
    private $coloursAvailable = array(
        Vehicle::BLUE, Vehicle::BLACK, Vehicle::RED, Vehicle::WHITE);

    private $carsInStock = array();

    public function __construct() {
        // If data file exists load it into $carsInStock
        if (file_exists(CarModel::DB_FILE)):
            $this->carsInStock =
                unserialize(file_get_contents(
                                    CarModel::DB_FILE));
        endif;
    }

    public function getCarTypesAvailable() {
```

```
            return $this->carTypesAvailable;
        }

        public function getEngineSizesAvailable() {
            return $this->engineSizesAvailable;
        }

        public function getColoursAvailable() {
            return $this->coloursAvailable;
        }

        public function getCarsInStock() {
            return $this->carsInStock;
        }

        public function addCarToStock($car_type, $engine_size, $colour) {
            $engine = new StandardEngine($engine_size);
            $car = new $car_type($engine, $colour);
            array_push($this->carsInStock, $car);
            file_put_contents(CarModel::DB_FILE,
                             serialize($this->carsInStock));
        }

    }
```

The graphical display is performed by the View. It takes a reference to the Model in its constructor so that it can ask the model for the data it needs to show. It also makes use of a separate "view template" PHP file which contains the HTML itself, and uses a session variable to store the view object so that the template can gain access to it:

car_view.php

```
    class CarView {

        // The view needs a reference to the model
        private $model;

        public function __construct(CarModel $model) {
            $this->model = $model;
            $_SESSION['view'] = serialize($this);
        }

        public function getModel() {
            return $this->model;
        }

        public function output() {
            require_once('car_view_template.php');
            $_SESSION['view'] = serialize($this);
            header('Location: car_view_template.php');
```

```php
            die();
        }

    }
```

car_view_template.php

```php
<?php
require_once('imports.php');
session_start();
$view = unserialize($_SESSION['view']);
?>
<html>
    <body>
        <h1>Car Management</h1>

        <h2>Add to stock</h2>
        <form name="add_to_stock" function="post" action="index.php">
            <p>
                Type:
                <select name="selected_car_type">
                    <?php foreach
                        ($view->getModel()->getCarTypesAvailable()
                        as $car_type): ?>
                        <option value="<?php echo $car_type; ?>">
                            <?php echo $car_type; ?>
                        </option>
                    <?php endforeach; ?>
                </select>
                Engine:
                <select name="selected_engine_size">
                    <?php foreach
                        ($view->getModel()->getEngineSizesAvailable()
                        as $engine_size): ?>
                        <option value="<?php echo $engine_size; ?>">
                            <?php echo $engine_size; ?>
                        </option>
                    <?php endforeach; ?>
                </select>
                Colour:
                <select name="selected_car_type">
                    <?php foreach
                        ($view->getModel()->getColoursAvailable()
                        as $colour): ?>
                        <option value="<?php echo $colour; ?>">
                            <?php echo $colour; ?>
                        </option>
                    <?php endforeach; ?>
                </select>
            </p>
        </form>

        <h2>Cars in stock</h2>
        <ul>
```

```
                    <?php foreach($view->getModel()->getCarsInStock()
                                                         as $car): ?>
                        <li><?php echo $car; ?></li>
                    <?php endforeach; ?>
                </ul>
            </body>
        </html>
```

Note: `imports.php` specifies `require_once` for each of the PHP files in this section.

The `Controller` class is responsible for handling the user input, which in this case is the **Submit** button to add a car to the stock list. All the controller needs to do is tell the model to add a car and then tell the view that it needs to redisplay itself:

car_controller.php

```
class CarController {

    // Need a reference to both the model and the view
    private $model;
    private $view;

    public function __construct(CarModel $model, CarView $view) {
        $this->model = $model;
        $this->view = $view;
    }

    public function submitPressed($car_type, $engine_size, $colour) {
        $this->model->addCarToStock($car_type, $engine_size, $colour);
        $this->view->output();
    }

}
```

The application itself is launched from a "front controller", in this case simply an `index.php` file:

index.php

```
<?php
include_once('imports.php'); // includes all PHP files
session_start();

$model = new CarModel();
$view = new CarView($model);
```

```
$controller = new CarController($model, $view);

if (isset($_POST['submit'])):
    // Submit button clicked on form
    $controller->submitClicked
               (filter_input(INPUT_POST, 'selected_car_type'),
                filter_input(INPUT_POST, 'selected_engine_size'),
                filter_input(INPUT_POST, 'selected_colour'));
else:
    // Initial page before first submission
    $view->output();
endif;
?>
```

A few final notes to clarify the MVC architecture:

- The *model* provides the main body of code, containing the business logic and state. It would also perform any data input validations and is independent of the view and controller;

- The *view* gets the data it needs to display from the model. This allows you to potentially create multiple views (e.g. one view as a tabular list and another view as a bar chart of the same data) where each view accesses the same model;

- The *controller* is "thin" in that it just responds to user interaction (such as button clicks), delegating the main work to the model. It can tell the view that it needs to update itself but it should <u>not</u> pass data to the view!

The example application given above, while adhering to the classical MVC architecture, has been kept deliberately simple to aid your understanding of the principles of the pattern. Once your application grows beyond the simple then the approach above becomes harder to scale, and therefore you should seriously consider utilising a pre-built PHP MVC framework that can take care of many of the complications for you. A few sample free open-source MVC frameworks are listed below:

- CakePHP - http://cakephp.org
- CodeIgniter - http://ellislab.com/codeigniter
- FuelPHP - http://www.fuelphp.com
- Symfony - http://symfony.com

- Yii - http://www.yiiframework.com
- Zend Framework - http://framework.zend.com

A more sophisticated implementation of MVC known as Hierarchical MVC (HMVC) can further help in scaling larger applications (particularly web applications), by allowing multiple MVC "triads" to be structured into parent-child hierarchies. Again, using a dedicated framework that supports HMVC would be recommended over trying to write one yourself from scratch.

Part VI. Appendixes

This part contains the appendixes, which includes a brief explanation of the Unified Modeling Language (UML) diagram formats for those unfamiliar with UML, and a quick reference for each of the 23 main patterns.

Appendix A. UML Diagrams

This book uses a simplified version of Unified Modeling Language (UML) diagrams to illustrate class hierarchies and usages for the patterns in this book. Each separate class is shown as a bounded rectangle with three horizontal sections, the top section containing the name of the class, the second section any relevant state (i.e. instance variables) and the third section containing the protocol (i.e. functions).

Representing types

Abstract classes, interfaces and abstract functions are shown in italicised text. The following figure shows an example of each sort of type and function:

Class
$state
function1() function2()

AbstractClass
$state
concreteFunction() *abstractFunction()*

«interface» *Interface*
function1() *function2()*

Figure A.1 : Normal class (left), abstract class (centre), interface (right)

The majority of diagrams in this book omit the state, thus leaving a small gap between the two horizontal bars (see the interface example in Figure A.1). This should not be taken to mean there is no state in the actual class; rather that it would have cluttered the diagram unnecessarily. Likewise, only relevant functions are listed, and not necessarily all. Unless specified otherwise, you can assume that all listed functions are `public`.

Representing inheritance

Inheritance is shown by a line connection between classes, with a hollow triangle pointing to the class being inherited or interfaces being implemented. Solid lines are shown for classes and dashed lines for interface connections:

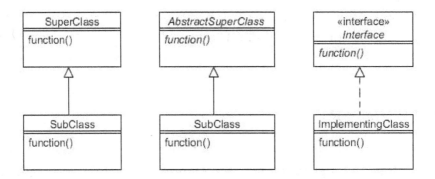

Figure A.2 : Extending a class (left & centre), implementing an interface (right)

Representing composition and usage

When one class 'uses' another (i.e. holds a reference to it), this is shown by a dashed line with an open arrow pointing toward the class being used. The usage is usually through passing a reference to the using object's constructor or a function, or by instantiating the object being used. In the following diagram each instance of ClassA holds or obtains a reference to an instance of ClassB:

Figure A.3 : ClassA uses ClassB

Code snippets

Where useful, snippets of code will be shown in a grey box attached to a class with a dashed line:

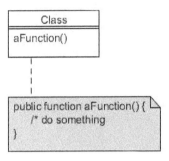

Figure A.4 : Code snippet

'Client' and other grey coloured classes

If a class rectangle is shown in grey this only for aesthetic purposes to separate it from other classes in the diagram. This is most often used in this book for 'client' classes, i.e. classes which make use of a particular pattern, as the following example for the *Chain of Responsibility* pattern illustrates:

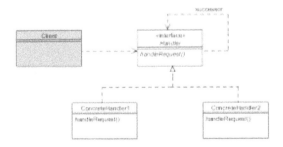

Figure A.5 : Client class in grey

Appendix B. Design Pattern Quick Reference

This appendix provides an alphabetical quick-reference of each of the 23 main design patterns described in this book in their most general form.

Note that many of the patterns make use of abstract classes or interfaces. In most cases these are interchangeable and the choice of which to use depends entirely upon your project requirements. It may also appear that the general form of a particular pattern described in this chapter differs from the detailed example in the main body of this book, but this is just a consequence of the fact that patterns are adaptable to the needs of the situation, and the general form should not be construed as the only or 'correct' approach.

Abstract Factory

Type	Creational
Purpose	Provide an interface for creating families of related or dependent objects without specifying their concrete classes.
Example usage	Commonly used when generating graphical 'widgets' for different look-and-feels.
Consequences	Isolates concrete classes. Enables easy exchange of product families. Promotes consistency among products.

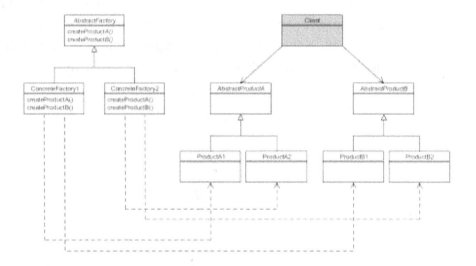

• `AbstractFactory` defines an interface for functions that create abstract product objects;

• `ConcreteFactory1` and `ConcreteFactory2` take care of instantiating the appropriate product families (e.g. `ConcreteFactory1` creates `ProductA1` and `ProductB1`);

• `AbstractProductA` and `AbstractProductB` defines the interface of each different type of product;

Client programs only use the interfaces declared by `AbstractFactory` and `AbstractProductA` and `AbstractProductB`.

Adapter

Type	Structural
Purpose	Convert the interface of a class into another interface clients expect. Adapter lets classes work together that couldn't otherwise because of incompatible interfaces.
Example usage	Integration of independent and incompatible classes.
Consequences	A single adapter can work with many adaptees.

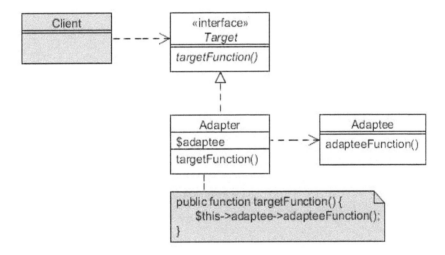

• Target refers to the interface that the client program requires;

• Adapter is the class used by client programs to forward requests to Adaptee;

• Adaptee is the class that needs adapting.

Bridge

Type	Structural
Purpose	Decouple an abstraction from its implementation so that each may vary independently.
Example usage	GUI frameworks and persistence frameworks.
Consequences	An implementation is not permanently bound to an interface, and can be switched at run-time.

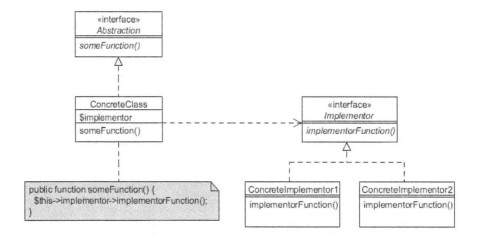

• Abstraction is the abstraction of the interface;

• ConcreteClass implements the Abstraction interface and holds a reference to Implementor. It provides an implementation in terms of Implementor;

• Implementor is the implementation interface which may be quite different to the Abstraction interface;

• ConcreteImplementor1 and ConcreteImplementor2 implement the Implementor interface.

Builder

Type	Creational
Purpose	Separate the construction of a complex object from its representation so that the same construction process can create different representations.
Example usage	Useful when there are several steps needed to create an object.
Consequences	Enables variations of a products internal representation. Isolates construction and representation.

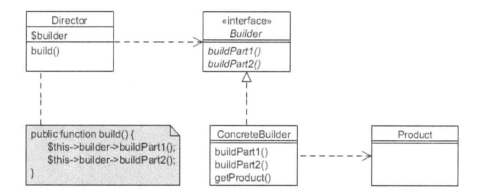

• `Builder` defines an interface for creating parts of a 'product' object;

• `ConcreteBuilder` creates and assembles the 'product' parts step-by-step and provides a function to retrieve it during or after assembly;

• `Director` controls the actual assembly process.

Chain of Responsibility

Type	Behavioural
Purpose	Avoid coupling the sender of a request to its receiver by giving more than one object a chance to handle the request. Chain the receiving objects and pass the request along the chain until an object handles it.
Example usage	When more than one object can handle a request and the handler is not known in advance.
Consequences	Not every request needs to be handled, or maybe it needs to be handled by more than one handler.

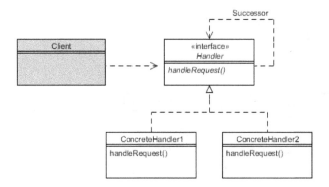

- `Handler` defines an interface for handling requests;

- `ConcreteHandler1` and `ConcreteHandler2` each decide if they can handle the request itself or if it should be passed on to its successor.

Client programs send their requests to the first object in the chain.

Command

Type	Behavioural
Purpose	Encapsulate a request as an object, thereby letting you parameterise clients with different requests, queue or log requests, and support undoable operations.
Example usage	UI controls such as menu items and toolbar buttons. Undo/redo mechanisms.
Consequences	Strive to keep separate the objects that invoke the operation from the object that performs it.

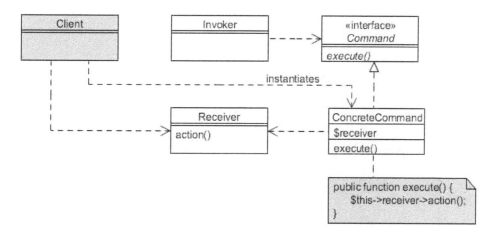

- Command is the interface for executing an operation;

- ConcreteCommand performs the operation on the Receiver;

- Invoker asks the command to be carried out;

- Receiver knows how to perform the operations.

Composite

Type	Structural
Purpose	Compose objects into tree structures to represent part-whole hierarchies. Composite lets clients treat individual objects and compositions of objects uniformly.
Example usage	Graphical component hierarchies, etc.
Consequences	Simple objects can be combined into complex assemblies and all treated through a common interface. Adding new components should be straightforward.

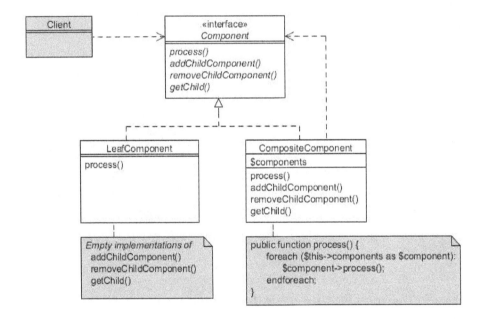

- `Component` is the interface for both leaves and composites;

- `LeafComponent` defines objects that have no children;

- `CompositeComponent` defines objects that may have children.

Decorator

Type	Structural
Purpose	Attach additional responsibilities to an object dynamically. Decorators provide a flexible alternative to subclassing for extending functionality.
Example usage	GUI toolkits file and object input/output streams (e.g. buffering).
Consequences	Can be more flexible than direct inheritance and reduce number of classes required.

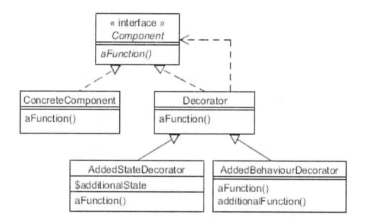

- Component defines the interface for objects that can have responsibilities added to them dynamically;

- ConcreteComponent implements the Component interface;

- Decorator maintains a reference to a Component object as well as defining an interface that matches that of Component;

- AddedStateDecorator and AddedBehaviourDecorator each decorate a Component by adding additional instance variables and/or functions.

Facade

Type	Structural
Purpose	Provide a unified interface to a set of interfaces in a subsystem. Facade defines a higher-level interface that makes the subsystem easier to use.
Example usage	To simplify access to several objects through a single 'facade' object.
Consequences	Needs a new class to be created to serve as the 'facade'.

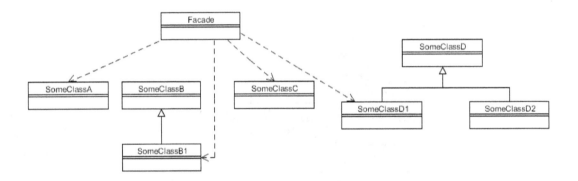

- **Facade** defines the class that provides the simplified interface to other classes;

- **SomeClassA**, *etc.* are various classes, related or not.

Factory Method

Type	Creational
Purpose	Define an interface for creating an object, but let subclasses decide which class to instantiate.
Example usage	When you can't anticipate the specific type of object to be created, or you want to localise the knowledge of which class gets created.
Consequences	Reduces the need for clients to use 'new' to instantiate objects.

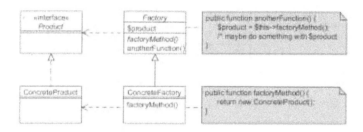

• Product defines the interface of the product that is to be created;

• ConcreteProduct is an implementation of a particular product;

• Factory declares the factory method that returns a Product object;

• ConcreteFactory implements the factory method defined in Factory to return an instance of Product.

Flyweight

Type	Structural
Purpose	Use sharing to support large numbers of fine-grained objects efficiently.
Example usage	Text/graphic editors, etc.
Consequences	Saves memory through sharing shared state.

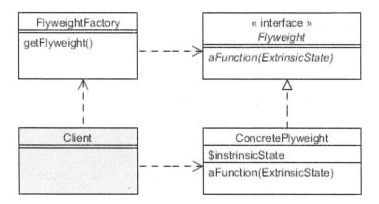

• `Flyweight` defines the interface through which flyweight objects can act on extrinsic state;

• `ConcreteFlyweight` implements `Flyweight` and stores intrinsic state. Must be shareable;

• `FlyweightFactory` creates and manages the flyweight objects through a 'pooling' mechanism.

Client programs maintain references to the flyweights obtained through the factory.

Interpreter

Type	Behavioural
Purpose	Given a language, define a representation for its grammar along with an interpreter that uses the representation to interpret sentences in the language.
Example usage	Simple grammars and mini-language processing.
Consequences	Not suitable for complex grammars and language processing.

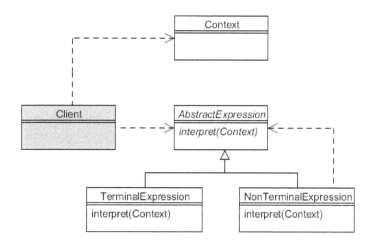

• `AbstractExpression` defines the abstract function to interpret an element;

• `TerminalExpression` extends `AbstractExpression` for language elements that terminate an expression;

• `NonTerminalExpression` extends `AbstractExpression` for language elements that are just part of an expression;

• `Context` is the object that is being parsed (e.g. the grammar or language).

Iterator

Type	Behavioural
Purpose	Provide a way to access the elements of an aggregate object sequentially without exposing its underlying representation.
Example usage	Wherever a collection or array of objects or values need to be processed in turn.
Consequences	The for-each syntax simplifies usage.

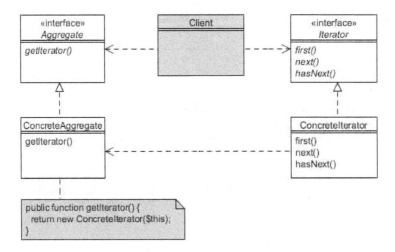

- Iterator defines the interface for the iterator;

- ConcreteIterator implements Iterator to perform the processing of each element in Aggregate;

- Aggregate defines the interface for the collection to be processed;

- ConcreteAggregate implements Aggregate for the actual collection.

Mediator

Type	Behavioural
Purpose	Define an object that encapsulates how a set of objects interact. Mediator promotes loose coupling by keeping objects from referring to each other explicitly, and it lets you vary their interaction independently.
Example usage	Dialogs that control UI components, etc.
Consequences	The Mediator could be defined to use the Observer pattern to monitor the components.

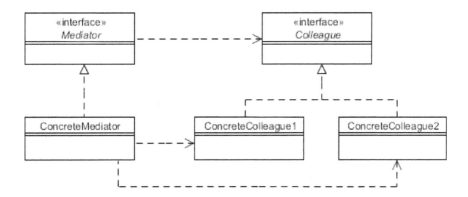

• `Mediator` defines the interface for communication with `Colleague` objects;

• `ConcreteMediator` implements the `Mediator` interface and performs the communication;

• `Colleague` defines the interface for a component that needs communication with the `Mediator`;

• `ConcreteColleague1` and `ConcreteColleague2` implement the `Colleague` interface and performs the communication with the `Mediator` such that it needs no knowledge of any other `Colleague`.

Memento

Type	Behavioural
Purpose	Without violating encapsulation, capture and externalise an object's internal state so that it can be restored to this state later.
Example usage	Undo & Redo processing, database transactions, etc.
Consequences	Encapsulates the storage of state external to the originating object, but might be expensive in terms of memory or performance.

- Originator creates the Memento object and uses it to restore its state;

- Memento stores the state of Originator;

- Caretaker keeps the memento.

Observer

Type	Behavioural
Purpose	Define a one-to-many dependency between objects so that when one object changes its state, all its dependants are notified and updated automatically.
Example usage	GUI controls, events, etc.
Consequences	Decouples classes through a common interface.

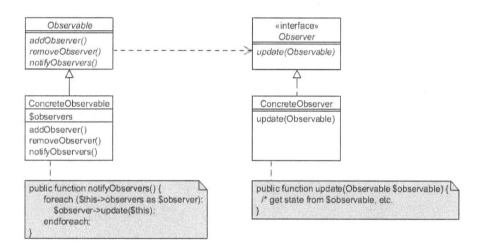

• `Observable` **defines the mechanisms to register observers and notify them of events;**

• `ConcreteObservable` **extends** `Observable` **for a particular subject class;**

• `Observer` **defines an interface for interested classes;**

• `ConcreteObserver` **implements** `Observer` **for a particular interested class.**

Prototype

Type	Creational
Purpose	Specify the kinds of objects to create using a prototypical instance, and create new objects by copying the prototype.
Example usage	Where easier or faster to clone than to instantiate.
Consequences	Cloning might become difficult in certain situations

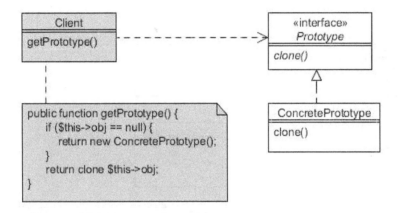

- Prototype defines an interface that can 'clone' itself;

- ConcretePrototype performs the self-cloning.

Client programs create new objects by asking a prototype to clone itself.

Proxy

Type	Structural
Purpose	Provide a surrogate or place-holder for another object to control access to it.
Example usage	Security proxies, etc.
Consequences	Performance may be impacted.

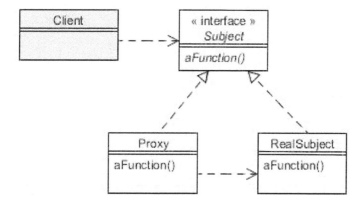

- Subject defines the interface that needs to be accessed through a proxy;

- RealSubject defines the actual object which Proxy represents;

- Proxy maintains a reference to RealSubject so it can act on its behalf.

Singleton

Type	Creational
Purpose	Ensure a class allows only one object to be created, providing a single point of access to it.
Example usage	Log files, configuration settings, etc.
Consequences	Often overused, difficult to subclass, can lead to tight coupling.

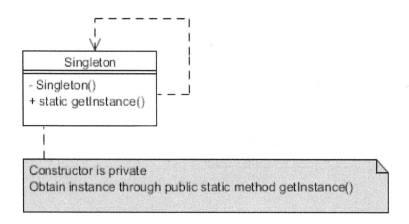

• `Singleton` defines a `private` constructor together with a `public` class (i.e. `static`) function as the only means of getting the instance.

Note that this book recommends using an `enum` to implement the *Singleton* pattern in most instances.

State

Type	Behavioural
Purpose	Allow an object to alter its behaviour when its internal state changes. The object will appear to change its class.
Example usage	UI shape components, etc.
Consequences	Localises state-specific behaviour and separates behaviour for different states.

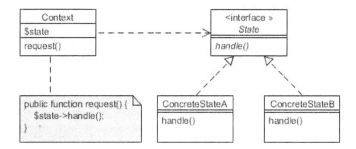

• `State` defines the interface for handling different states in the `handle()` function;

• `ConcreteStateA` and `ConcreteStateB` implement the `State` interface for each separate state;

• `Context` holds a reference to a `State` object to request a particular state.

Strategy

Type	Behavioural
Purpose	Define a family of algorithms, encapsulate each one, and make them interchangeable. Strategy lets the algorithm vary independently from clients that use it.
Example usage	Applying different cryptographic algorithms.
Consequences	Might need to pass data to each strategy.

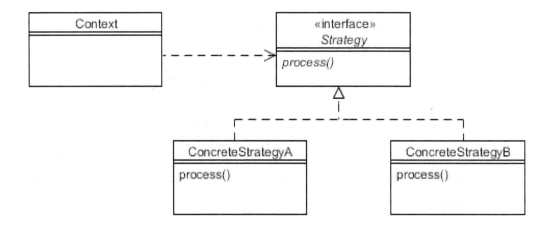

- `Strategy` defines the interface for the algorithms;

- `ConcreteStrategyA` and `ConcreteStrategyB` implement `Strategy` for a particular algorithm;

- `Context` holds a reference to the `Strategy` that is being used.

Template Method

Type	Behavioural
Purpose	Define the skeleton of an algorithm in a function, deferring some steps to subclasses. Template Method lets subclasses redefine certain steps of an algorithm without changing the algorithm's structure.
Example usage	When an algorithm's steps can be performed in different ways.
Consequences	Should prevent the template method from being overridden.

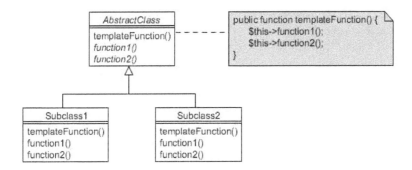

- AbstractClass defines the non-overridable templateFunction() that invokes a series of abstract functions defined in subclasses;

- Subclass1 and Subclass2 extend AbstractClass to define the code for each abstract function invoked by templateFunction().

Visitor

Type	Behavioural
Purpose	Represent a function to be performed on the elements of an object structure. Visitor lets you define a new function without changing the classes of the elements on which it operates.
Example usage	Similar operations need performing on different types in a structure, or as a means to add functionality without extensive modifications.
Consequences	Adding new visitable objects can require modifying visitors.

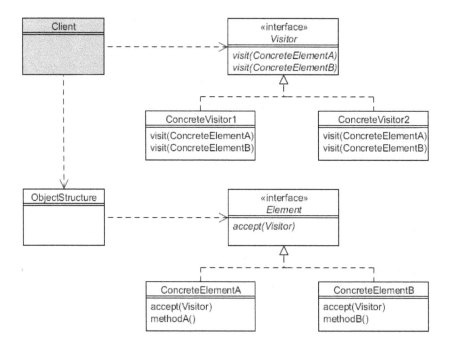

- Visitor defines the interface that declares functions to visit each kind of visitable Element;

- ConcreteVisitor1 and ConcreteVisitor2 implement the Visitor interface for each element that could be visited;

- Element defines the interface for all classes which could be visited;

- `ConcreteElementA` and `ConcreteElementB` implement the `Element` interface for each class that could be visited.

- `ObjectStructure` contains references to all objects that can be visited, enabling iteration through them.

Appendix C. Bibliography

Beck, Kent. *Extreme programming explained; Embrace Change.* Reading, MA: Addison-Wesley, 1999.

Fowler, Martin, et al. *Refactoring: improving the design of existing code.* River, NJ: Addison-Wesley, 2000.

Fowler, Martin, and Kendall Scott. *UML distilled, second edition: a brief guide to the standard object modeling language.* River, NJ: Addison-Wesley, 1999.

Gamma, Erich, et al. *Design patterns: elements of reusable object-oriented software.* River, NJ: Addison-Wesley, 1995.

Laney, Robin, et al. *Software engineering with objects.* Milton Keynes, The Open University, 2008.

Index